I0442237

1.0   Introduction

As part of Task 2.1.3, Effects on Aquatic Organisms, Subtask 2.1.3.1 is focused on evaluating the potential effects of electromagnetic field (EMF) exposure on fish and invertebrates. This report documents the preliminary results of experiments conducted in fiscal years (FY) 2010 and 2011. Because so little is known about the effects of EMF exposure on marine and estuarine fish and invertebrates, the Pacific Northwest National Laboratory (PNNL) project team employed an exploratory screening approach that evaluated a wide variety of fish and invertebrate species likely to be exposed to EMF during some part of their life stage.

The assessments were conducted under controlled laboratory conditions to reduce non-treatment effects, and generally followed existing toxicology and behavioral ecology protocols whenever possible. EMF field strengths and experimental exposures were intentionally designed to represent the upper bounds of expected exposures in field settings and to focus primarily on sublethal endpoints that could contribute to changes at an individual level that may ultimately influence community and population trends. It was assumed that a lack of a detectible response in the assessments would suggest adverse effects to these species were unlikely. However, interpretation of these results needs to account for experimental design and a variety of other factors that affect statistical power and contribute to uncertainty, including limits on test system configurations, availability of test organisms, replication of results, and finite time and financial resources.

Section 2 of this report provides a description of the Helmholtz coil system that was used to generate the electromagnetic fields used in the experiments and experimental design considerations with respect to the Helmholtz coil. Sections 3 and 4 provide the approach, assumptions, methods, and results for fish and invertebrate experiments, respectively. Sections 3 and 4 also include a discussion of statistical power and uncertainty with regard to test design, when appropriate, to place experimental results in context. Section 5 provides a discussion of the overall results and planned activities for aquatic organism assessments in Year 3 (FY 2012) of the project. Literature cited is presented in Section 6.

2.0   Helmholtz Coil Exposure System

During the initial stages of the project, the PNNL team reviewed relevant scientific literature to assess the existing state of knowledge concerning potential EMF effects on aquatic species. PNNL also worked closely with Oak Ridge National Laboratory (ORNL) to evaluate likely EMF emissions from tidal, wave buoy, and offshore wind deployments. Although limited, the information suggested that biological effects were possible at magnetic field strengths ranging from approximately 0.008 to 3.7 millitesla (mT) (Lerchel et al. 1998; Skauli et al. 2000; Bochert and Zettler 2004; Gill et al. 2009). Peer-reviewed literature and technical reports also suggested that in some cases, the EMF strength of experimental systems was either uncertain or highly variable because systems employed small rare-earth magnets or electromagnets that produced a non-uniform exposure field. Similar uncertainty existed with regard to expected EMF strengths for tidal, wave, and offshore wind ocean energy deployments.

In February 2010, ORNL contacted 10 marine and hydrokinetic (MHK) energy developers and research institutions requesting information on expected EMF levels that would be produced by their technologies. In all cases, responding organizations indicated they had not measured or predicted EMF for their devices or related power cables. However, ORNL was able to calculate expected field strengths from available information on amperage and cable properties; the calculated values suggest magnetic flux densities could range from 400 to more than 8,000 microtesla (μT) at the surface of the cable, or 0.4 to 8 mT (Cada et al. 2011). Field observations during the COWRIE EMF project indicated field strengths could range from 0.23 to 0.6 μT at the Burbo site and 0.01 μT at the Ardtow site (Gill et al. 2009). While these data suggest that EMF strengths from MHK devices could be low, they also illustrate that there is a high degree of uncertainty and variability related to actual field strengths that are likely to occur during MHK device operation..

To ensure consistent EMF exposures during experimental testing, PNNL procured a specialized Helmholtz coil system capable of producing a uniform EMF in a laboratory setting . The system can operate in either alternating current (AC) or direct current (DC) configurations and is capable of generating uniform fields ranging from approximately 0.1 to 3 mT; the highest EMF strengths are obtained in the DC configuration. These field strengths are expected to represent upper bounding conditions of likely emissions from MHK devices and cable systems, based on measurements taken in the field. A description of the Helmholtz coil system and examples of the Helmholtz and single coil configurations used during the project to evaluate potential EMF effects on marine, estuarine, and freshwater species are provided in the following subsections.

2.1   System Description and Design Considerations

The Helmholtz coil system used to support biological effects testing was purchased from Walker LDJ Scientific, Lake Orion, Michigan, in early 2010. The device consists of two square frames measuring 1.5 m (5 ft) on each side with an external 750-W power supply capable of operating in both AC and DC mode (Figure 2.1).

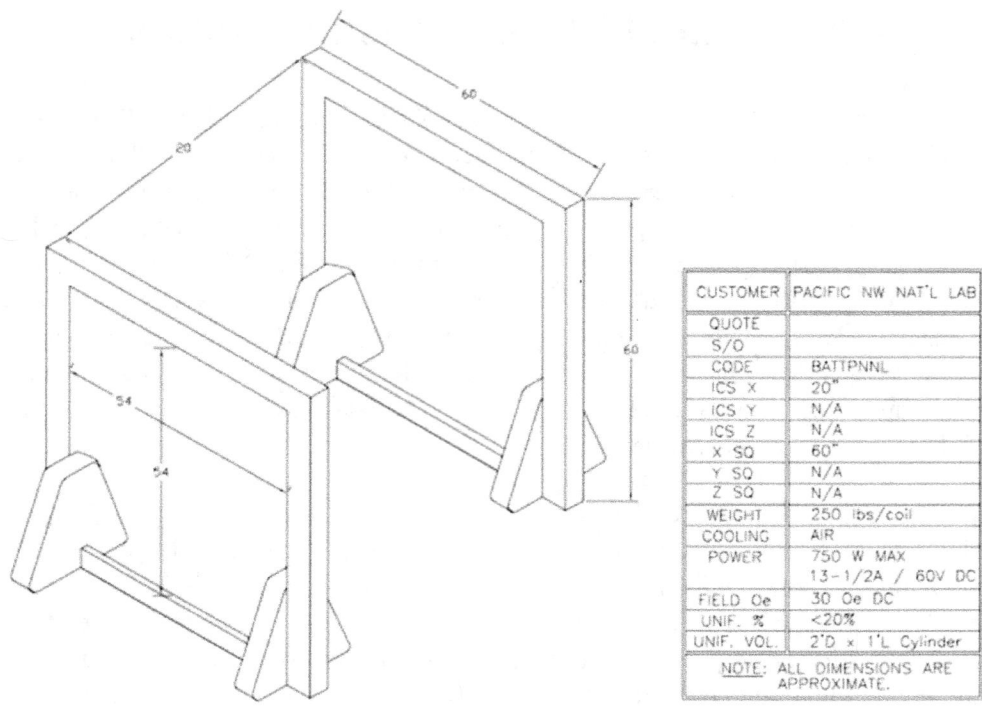

Figure 2.1. Helmholtz Coil Dimensions and Specifications

Initial EMF experiments focusing on organism survival, growth, and behavior were conducted in the Helmholtz configuration, with two coils parallel and a fixed distance apart (Figure 2.1). Prior to use in testing, the EMF field generated by the Helmholtz coils was mapped to verify the uniformity of field in the test area between the coils and to quantify field strength. The test area was approximately 61 cm wide × 152 cm long × 102 cm high (24 in. wide × 60 in. long × 40 in. high). A grid was established at 10.2-cm (4-in.) intervals vertically and horizontally, and EMF strength was determined using a Holaday HI-3550 magnetic field monitor. A three-dimensional image depicting field strength (Figure 2.2) inside and outside the test area was generated using the MATLAB software 3D plotting function (The MathWorks Inc., Natick, Massachusetts). The highest field strength generated was along the axes of where the coils were positioned; the average field strength within the effective testing area was 3.2 ± 0.13 mT. The resulting uniform field within the test area met our stated requirements for exposure effects testing, thereby reducing the quantification uncertainty related to biological exposures noted in the literature.

The uniform electromagnetic testing field was amenable to test configurations accommodating individual organisms in test chambers (i.e., antennular flicking responses of Dungeness crab) or multiple organisms in a larger test chamber (e.g., multiple numbers of small fish). Examples are shown in Section 2.2.1. To accommodate avoidance/attraction response testing with Dungeness crab this past year, the coils were separated and reconfigured, such that a decaying EMF was produced on either side of a coil. This configuration allowed one energized coil to be used as the treatment and the other non-energized coil to be used as the control. Using this configuration, the energized coil produced a maximum effective field intensity in the center of the tank (Figure 2.3 – EMF Exposure Tank) of 1.1 ± 0.1 mT, decaying to levels approximately three times the control tank intensities at either end of the tank (0.33 ± 0.1 mT). The control tank had EMF levels of approximately 0.12 ± 0.01 mT (Figure 2.3 – Control Tank).

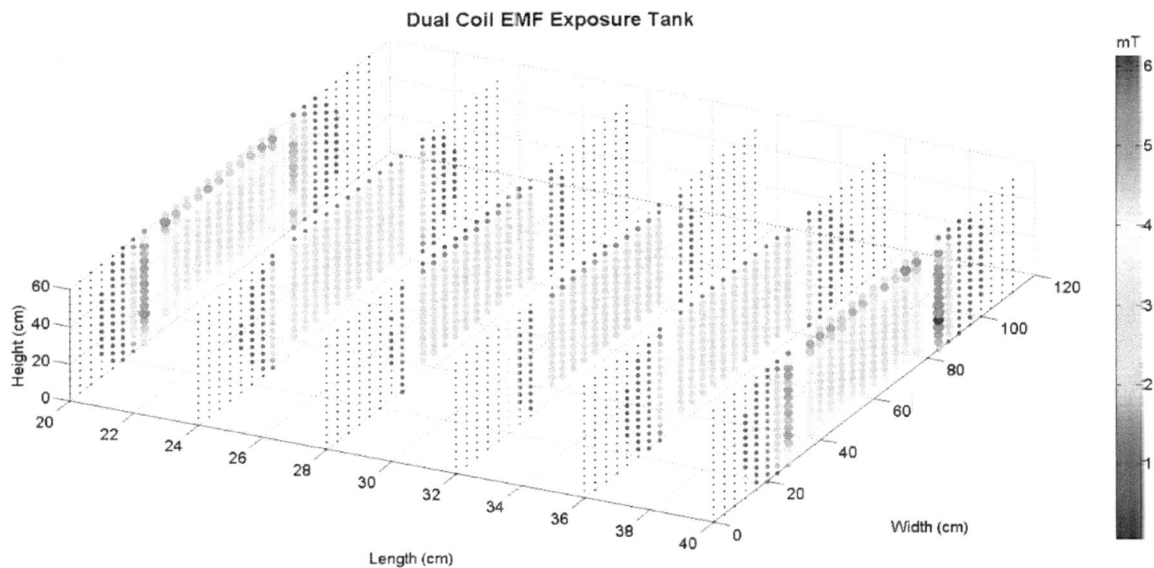

Figure 2.2. EMF Generated as millitesla (mT) in the Helmholtz (Dual-Coil) Configuration

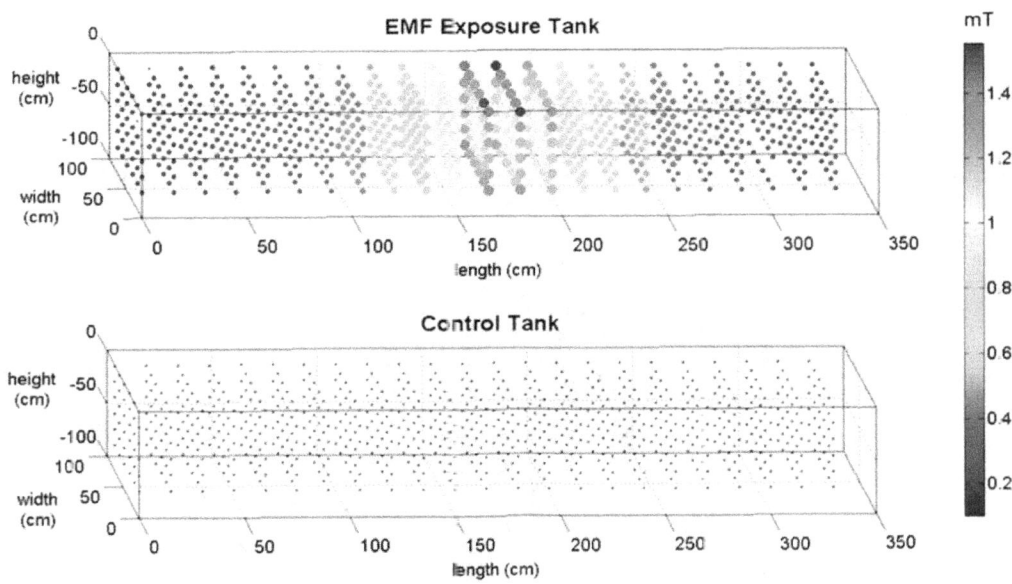

Figure 2.3. EMF Generated as millitesla (mT) in Single-Coil Configuration

The Helmholtz coil provided a uniform testing field where the level and degree of exposure could be accurately controlled. However, by necessity and design, the assessments and experiments we conducted were exploratory in nature (e.g., a wide range of species tested, biologically relevant endpoints not always apparent). In addition, the limitations imposed by a single (rather than multiple) test system and associated time constraints required modifications to the experimental design that ideally incorporates randomness, independence, and replication in a rigorous testing manner (Cochran and Cox, 1957). In our case, the ability to replicate treatment exposures in some circumstances (e.g. an extended-time exposure of multiple fish in one tank) was compromised, thus reducing a measure of true variability. Increased replication would allow an increase in statistical power, and thus a greater likelihood of detecting a biologically relevant effect as statistically significant. The EMF strengths we tested were designed to represent the upper bounds of field exposures. Thus any responses we observed would be expected to be reduced at lower EMF intensities.

2.2 Test System Examples

2.2.1 Helmholtz Configuration

As described above, initial EMF experiments were conducted using the Helmholtz configuration to ensure a uniform magnetic field within the experimental enclosures. In this configuration, tanks containing test organisms were positioned between the coils on an elevated platform to ensure all organisms received the same EMF exposure. Examples of the Helmholtz configuration used for fish and invertebrate testing are provided in Figures 2.4 through 2.7. Because ancillary stimuli not directly associated with the experimental treatments (i.e., sound, personnel movement, extraneous lighting) could interfere with behavioral testing results, a temporary wall was constructed around the Helmholtz system to isolate it from the rest of the laboratory, and individual test chambers were isolated using black plastic sheeting or physical barriers, depending on the experimental design. In addition, all behavioral tests were video recorded to permit detailed analyses after the experiments were completed and to provide visual documentation of test results (Figure 2.8).

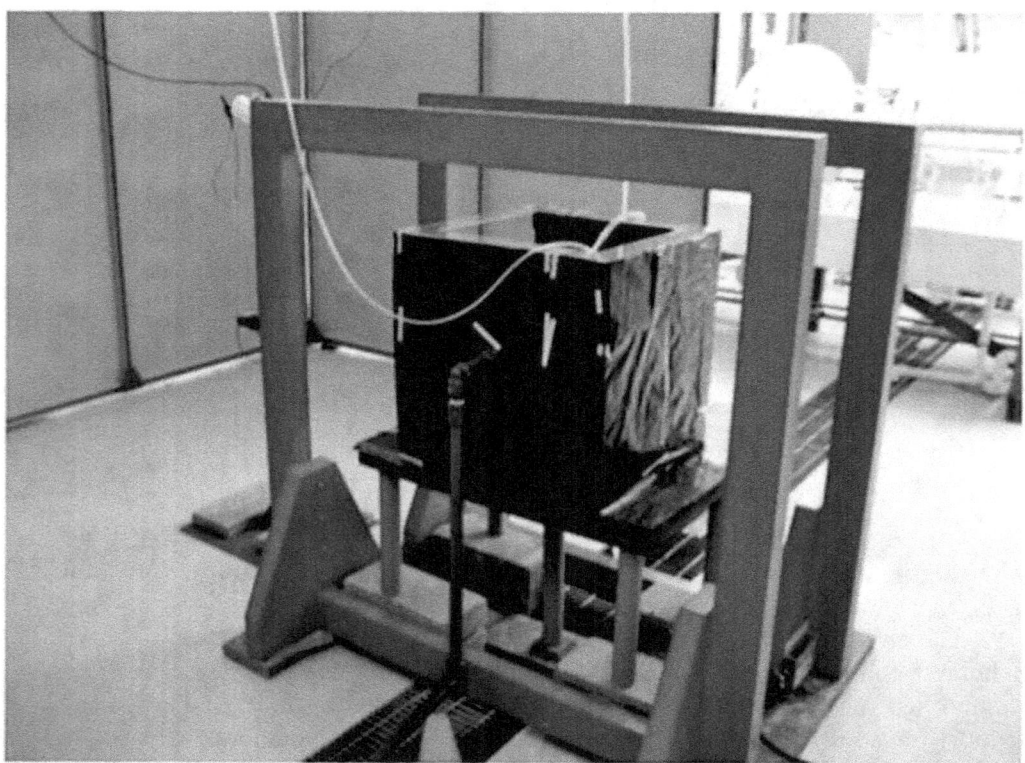

Figure 2.4. Experimental System for Coho Salmon and Atlantic Halibut

Figure 2.5. Experimental System for California Halibut

Figure 2.6. Experimental System for Rainbow Trout

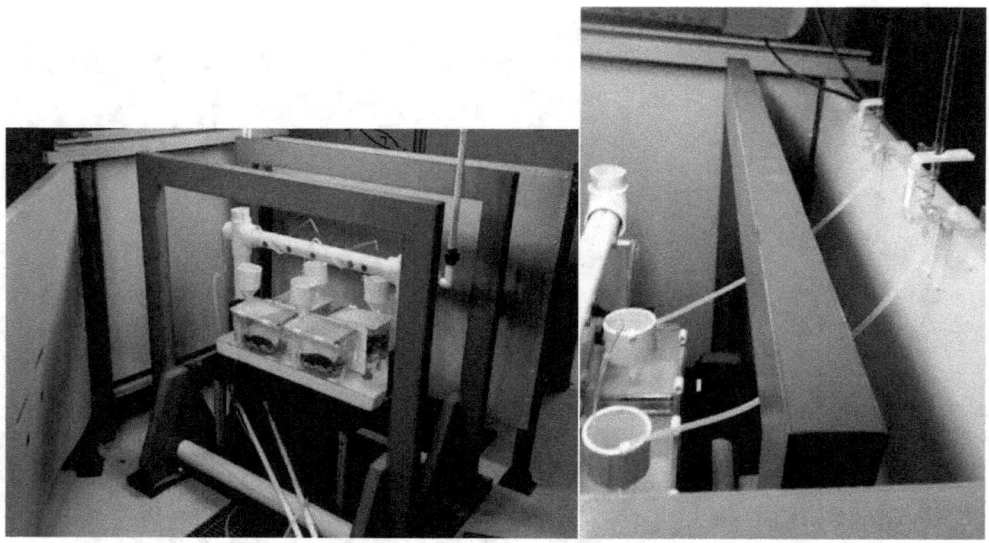

Figure 2.7. Experimental System for Dungeness Crab Antennular Flicking (left) and Modification of Buret Delivery System for Food Detection (right)

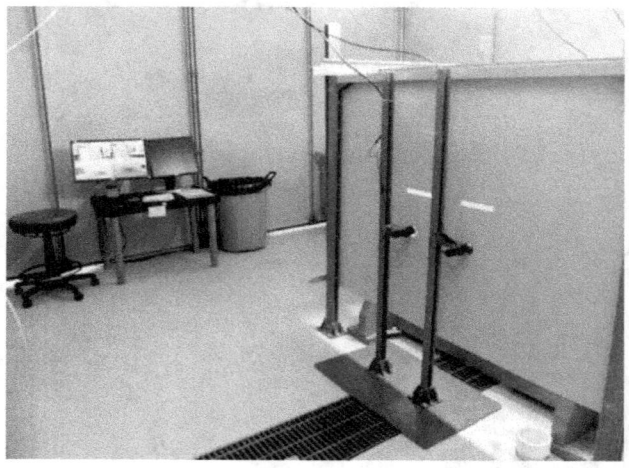

Figure 2.8. Recording System and Visual Blinds Placed Around Helmholtz Coil and Experimental System Shown in Figure 2.7

2.2.2   Single-Coil Configuration

The Helmholtz coil configuration was modified for the avoidance/attraction experiments with Dungeness crab. In this configuration, one energized coil was positioned at the midpoint of a rectangular tank to serve as the treatment test system. A short distance away but outside the EMF field effects, a second non-energized coil was positioned over an identical tank to provide a control exposure (Figure 2.9). As described above, a video-capture system was used for both tanks to record test organism behavior.

Figure 2.9. Control and EMF Exposure Tanks for Dungeness Crab Avoidance/Attraction Experiments

3.0 Fish Experiments

3.1 Introduction

This subtask is investigating the effects of EMF on marine and freshwater fishes. A literature search, prior to the initiation of experiments, indicated relatively little had been published on the effects of EMF on fishes. However, three studies, based on rigorous experimental designs, suggested possible effects. Skauli et al. (2000) observed a delay in zebrafish (*Danio rerio*) embryogenesis after exposure to a 1-mT EMF (AC current, 50 Hz). The EMF was generated using Helmholtz coils of a design similar to that described in Section 2 (although smaller in scale). This finding is in general agreement with those observed using other non-fish vertebrate models that suggest EMF exposure can alter the timing of developmental processes (Juutilainen 2005). Lerchl et al. (1998) reported that brook trout (*Salvelinus fontinalis*) exposed for 45 min to a 0.04-mT EMF (pulsing DC current, 800 ms off and 200 ms on) significantly increased the nighttime melatonin levels in both plasma and the pineal gland. This study also used Helmholtz coils for EMF generation. This finding is interesting as it is in general agreement with the "melatonin hypothesis" (Reiter 1995) that EMF can alter melatonin secretion, but it differs in that typically EMF exposure reduces melatonin levels (Stevens and Davis 1996). Gill et al. (2009) observed that a weak EMF (0.008 mT) produced by a simulated underwater power cable significantly altered swimming patterns of catsharks (*Scyliorhinus canicula*) held in large estuarine enclosures. Although these are three independent fish studies, they collectively suggest the potential for EMF to influence select developmental, physiological, and behavioral processes in sensitive fishes. With so little known about potential EMF effects of MHK devices, our experimental approach was designed to both expand and confirm the findings of previous studies using fish species representative of those important to MHK stakeholders.

3.1.1 Testing Goals and Objectives

Testing goals and objectives were as follows:

- Determine the potential for adverse developmental effects related to EMF exposure to a variety of salmonid and flatfish species. The goal is to provide information on the potential for EMF exposure to affect growth and development or to invoke behavioral changes that could affect species spatial or temporal distribution, predator-prey relationships, or food-web dynamics.

- Develop a rapid, screening-level assessment of the effects of EMF on a range of organisms in the laboratory and recommend organisms for in depth dose–response experiments.

3.1.2 Species Selection

Fish species selection was based on relevance with regard to the endpoints to be measured, availability, and existence of established methods for laboratory culturing. EMF impacts on fish development processes were studied at three different life history stages: embryogenesis and larval– juvenile and parr–smolt transformations. For the embryogenesis studies, rainbow trout were selected based on the principal investigator's past experience (Schultz et al. 2003, 2008; Brown et al. 2007). For the larval–juvenile studies, flatfish metamorphosis was chosen as the model system. Atlantic halibut (*Hippoglossus hippoglossus*) and California halibut (*Paralichthys californicus*) were selected as the test species because both are found in areas of planned or existing MHK sites and are cultured commercially.

In addition, both have well-characterized developmental staging and, therefore, are good model organisms to use for these experiments (Gisbert et al. 2002; Saele et al. 2004). The parr–smolt transformation and initial behavioral and physiological studies used coho salmon (*Oncorhynchus kisutch*).

3.1.3　Rationale for Experimental Designs

Many fishes, such as rainbow trout (*O. mykiss*) and coho salmon (*O. kisutch*) possess magnetic-field sensing magnetite (Fe_3O_4) crystals that are concentrated in the snout or anterior head region (Wiltschko and Wiltschko 2005; Hellinger and Hoffmann 2009). The highest concentration of these crystals is typically associated with the olfactory lamellae and trigeminal nerve, which provides neuronal inputs to the hippocampus and other higher brain regions. This implies a connection between magnetic field perception, olfaction, and memory or imprinting of a stimulus (e.g., predator odor). Demersal fishes such as flatfish have a complex life history involving a symmetrical free-swimming larval stage and an asymmetrical post-larval juvenile–adult stage. Demersal fishes are anticipated to receive higher EMF exposures in the field due to their benthic life style, which may place them near MHK transmission cables unless an active avoidance behavior is present. Physiological or hormonal markers of exposure were tested in coho salmon and focused on plasma cortisol and melatonin levels. Cortisol is an established stress response marker and is known to participate in the parr–smolt transformation (Bjornsson et al. 2011). Similarly, melatonin is well characterized in coho salmon and also involved in smoltification of salmonids (Gern et al. 1984).

3.2　Coho Salmon Alarm-Response

During FY 2010 and FY 2011, experiments were conducted to determine if exposure to EMF affected the ability of coho salmon to detect alarm odorants that are used to detect the presence of predators. Follow-on experiments were conducted in early FY 2011, as described below. Inhibition of predator detection following exposure to EMF could significantly affect survivability of both juvenile and adult salmon, resulting in potential effects at community and population levels if the likelihood of exposure were high and comprised a significant number of individuals.

3.2.1　Methods

For behavioral studies, juvenile coho salmon (approximately 15 cm [5.9 in.] fork length) were exposed to EMF and then stimulated with an anti-predatory alarm substance to determine if their predator avoidance behavior had been affected by EMF exposure. This response has been used by the National Oceanic and Atmospheric Administration (NOAA) Fisheries and others (Stone et al. 1994; Brown and Smith 1997; Scholz et al. 2000; Tierney et al. 2006) to determine if exposure to chemicals from stormwater or other sources affects the predator-avoidance behavior of these fish. For EMF exposures, each experiment was conducted using one to five hatchery-reared juvenile salmon that had been acclimated in exposure cubes for 7 days. One cube receiving EMF exposure was designated as the test exposure; an identical cube placed outside the influence of the Helmholtz coil system served as the control exposure. Following acclimation, the fish were exposed to a static 3-mT field for 1 to 14 days. An anti- predatory alarm substance consisting of 10 mL of homogenized coho salmon skin was added to each tank through a remote syringe apparatus, and fish response was monitored by the video cameras. The rationale for this test was based on work by Tierney et al. (2006) whereby a predator attacks a fish and causes skin damage, releasing a variety of endogenous chemicals into the water that alerts other individuals of a predator's presence. The type of behavioral response elicited can vary among fishes, but in juvenile coho salmon, the expected response is initial darting or rapid swimming followed by cessation of swimming and "freezing" behavior.

3.2.2   Results

Under non-stressed conditions, coho salmon were expected to swim throughout the water column. When the alarm substance was added, the fish were expected to become motionless until the alarm substance was diluted by clean water inflow and cleared from the cube (Brown and Smith 1997). Four experiments were conducted in which the salmon were exposed to EMF for varying lengths of time and then introduced to the predatory alarm substance. During the first two experiments, the alarm substance was introduced during the daytime hours when the lights were on. Throughout the exposure, the fish remained situated primarily at the bottom of the test and exposure cubes and moved very little within the water column prior to and after the alarm substance was introduced. This response indicated the fish were displaying the stereotypical avoidance behaviors constantly throughout the experiment, possibly in reaction to the small size of the cubes required to fit within the Helmholtz coil configuration or to other nontreatment stressors.

Through video monitoring of the non-EMF exposed control cube under non-stressed conditions, fish were observed to be more active at night when the lights were off. For this reason, the original protocol was altered to add the alarm substance 30 min after the lights went off instead of during the day. The experiments in the dark conditions provided variable results.

During the third trial, fish were exposed to EMF 5 days prior to the addition of the predator stimulus. The skin extract was added to the cubes 30 min after dark, and fish were monitored for the behavior. Before the extract was added, fish were observed swimming in the water column at various depths within the test and control cubes. Immediately after the extract was added, the fish displayed noticeable defensive behavior—schooling at the bottom of each cube, becoming increasingly motionless, and aligning themselves into the flow of water. This behavior lasted 30–60 min following stimulus addition; the fish returned to the full water column once the alarm substance was cleared from the cubes. For this trial, the observed behavioral response suggested that exposure to EMF did not inhibit the alarm response in coho salmon.

During the fourth trial, fish were exposed to 1 day of EMF and the stimulus was added 30 min after dark. In the video footage, the fish appeared to be displaying an alarm response both prior to and after the addition of the skin extract. It is possible the variability in behavior between trials three and four could be due to human disturbances prior to the addition of the alarm substance, despite precautions taken to reduce non-treatment responses through the use of physical barriers and limiting fish view through exposure containers. Because the fish respond to light cues, adding the alarm substance in the dark with low-level auxiliary lighting may have created shadows that were interpreted as predator movement by the test and control fish.

A subsequent experiment used juvenile coho of smaller size (approximately 7 cm [2.8 in.] fork length) to assess whether better acclimation to the exposure system would occur. However, results similar to those found using the larger fish were obtained. At this point, further coho salmon behavioral testing was stopped, as it did not appear tractable under the restrictions imposed by the exposure system.

3.3 Coho Salmon Exposure Markers

Measurement of exposure markers was pursued using coho salmon as a means to detect underlying physiological changes that may precede more overt responses at the whole-organism level. Exposure marker testing was done using short-term EMF exposures that allowed testing of a variety of exposure levels and currents (AC and DC).

3.3.1 Methods

3.3.1.1 Fish

Juvenile coho salmon were obtained from NOAA Northwest Fisheries Science Center (Seattle, Washington). The fish were initially transported to the Marine Sciences Laboratory (MSL; Sequim, Washington) in freshwater. After 3 months of acclimation at MSL, the fish were then smolted by gradually raising the salinity 5–7 ppt per week, until full-strength seawater was obtained. After 2 months of seawater acclimation, the fish were then used in subsequent EMF experiments. At this time, the fish varied in weight between 150 and 250 g (5.3 and 8.8 oz).

3.3.1.2 Exposure Protocol and Cortisol and Melatonin Measurements

All EMF exposures lasted 80 hr. For each EMF exposure, four fish were placed in the acrylic experimental cubes (0.6 m× 0.6 m × 0.6 m [2 ft × 2 ft × 2 ft]) filled with 40–50 L (10.5–13.2 gal) of filtered Sequim Bay seawater supplied via a flow-through system. Temperatures were maintained between 9°C and 10°C (48–50°F), and water flow rates ranged between 2 and 4 L/min. One cube was situated in the center of the Helmholtz coils, and one cube was set up 6.1 m (20 ft) away, outside of measurable EMF generated by the Helmholtz coils. A concurrent control group was sampled for each treatment. The fish were exposed to measured EMF levels of 0.1 and 3 mT, generated using DC electrical current. These exposure levels were repeated using a pulsed EMF generated every 2 sec (on/off cycle) to verify the response reported in brook trout (Lerchl et al. 1998), which used a similar type of EMF exposure (0.044 mT DC, 0.2 s on and 0.8 s off). A fifth EMF exposure was performed using a field intensity of 0.13 mT generated using AC electrical current operated at 40 Hz. The EMF exposure concluded at 12:00 a.m. (0000 hr). Fish were euthanized with tricaine methanesulfonate (MS-222; 250 mg/L); a blood sample was obtained from the caudal vein, and the plasma was separated by centrifugation ($3,000 \times g$ for 5 min). Plasma sampling took approximately 4 min per fish. All fish sampling was done in complete darkness. Fish handlers used headlamps fitted with red filters to prevent stimulation of the pineal gland. Both cortisol and melatonin were measured in plasma using commercially available ELISA kits (Neogen Inc.).

3.3.1.3 Statistical Analysis and Design Considerations

For this experiment, a one-sample t-test was used to evaluate the null hypothesis that the mean result from the EMF-treated tank is an observation from within the control distribution (i.e., has the same mean and variance as the controls). A Bonferroni correction was used because the same control data were being compared against more than one EMF treatment.

As a preliminary assessment, we chose to test several EMF treatment scenarios. However, due primarily to time constraints associated with the use of the Helmholtz coil, the subsequent lack of tank replication for each EMF treatment precluded a more robust statistical analysis. Although EMF exposures used a single tank, the fish inside were allowed to move freely, thus reducing tank-exposure effects. In addition, we replicated the control treatment, permitting alternative analysis to be conducted, thus avoiding the problem of confounded effects.

3.3.2 Results

3.3.2.1 Cortisol

Plasma cortisol levels were observed to vary substantially between the treatment groups. Mean values in the EMF treatments ranged from 235 to 1510 µg/L and varied from 382 to 1520 µg/L in the control groups. Visual inspection of the results did not identify any trends in the results, and the cortisol levels varied among individuals. There was no evidence of a statistically significant difference in cortisol production between exposed and non-exposed fish.

3.3.2.2 Melatonin

Mean plasma melatonin levels exhibited greater consistency among the control groups, varying between 33 and 49 pg/ml. In the EMF treatment groups, mean values were typically lower than those of control fish and varied between 1.5 and 34 pg/ml. A graphical summary of the results is shown in Figure 3.1 A and B (note that melatonin analysis in the 3-mT constant-on group has not been completed). Initial inspection of the biological variation within each tank (Figure 3.1 A) showed that the largest difference in melatonin levels was in the 3-mT on/off EMF exposure and relatively similar values were observed for the 0.1-mT EMF exposure. However, the 0.13-mT EMF (AC current) appeared to produce a change intermediate in scope. The one-sample t-test using the data shown in Figure 3.1 B indicated both the 3-mT constant on and 0.13-mT AC current have a low probability (multiple comparison error rate = 0.05; $p < 0.0125$) of being from the control distribution. Therefore, this preliminary assessment suggests EMF exposure may alter melatonin levels in fish and warrants further testing to confirm initial results. It is also interesting to note these results are consistent with those obtained from other vertebrate model systems, which have indicated EMF exposure suppresses nighttime melatonin production by the pineal gland (Steven and Davis 1996).

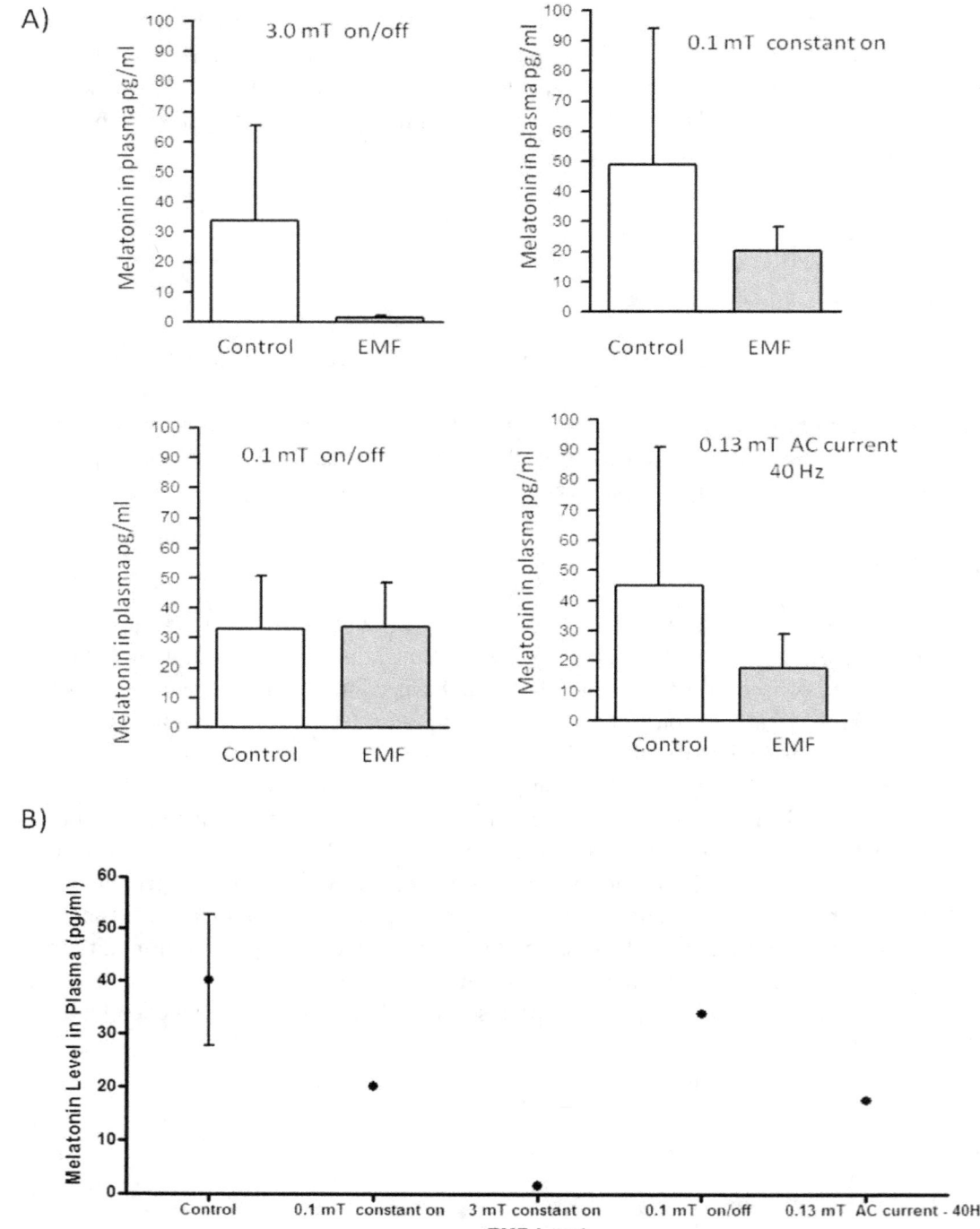

Figure 3.1. Nighttime Plasma Melatonin Levels in Juvenile Coho Salmon Exposed for 80 hr to Various EMF Levels. A) Biological variation within single tank replicates. The specific EMF treatment is indicated on each graph. Values are mean $\pm$ SD ($n = 4$ coho in each replicate). B) Overall summary at tank replicate level. The four separate control experiments are combined (mean and 95% confidence interval) and plotted against the mean values for each EMF exposure.

3.4   Rainbow Trout Egg Development

This experiment investigated the effects of EMF exposure on embryogenesis in rainbow trout, a species also under investigation by Oak Ridge National Laboratory. Two groups of fertilized trout eggs were exposed to a constant 3-mT EMF field ranging from 10 to 17 days, then examined to assess developmental progress. Concurrent control exposures without EMF were also conducted. Interference with normal egg development could result in death, delayed development, or greater susceptibility to predation, leading to both community and population-level effects if the potential for exposure were high and involved a large number of individuals. The likelihood of exposure will vary by species, with those depositing or burying eggs near transmission cables receiving the greatest potential exposure.

3.4.1   Methods

3.4.1.1   Egg Fertilization

Approximately 24 hr prior to the arrival of the rainbow trout eggs from a commercial fish hatchery (TroutLodge, Inc., Lacey, Washington), one individual male rainbow trout (of the OSU × Arlee strain) was stripped of semen. The semen was calculated to have an average sperm count of 1.793 million/μL. Sperm were stored at 4°C until arrival of rainbow trout eggs the following day. Eggs were fertilized at a ratio of 4.4×10^5 sperm cells/egg in 50-mL fertilization buffer (60 mM NaHCO3 and 50 mM TRIS). Twenty-five eggs were set aside as an unfertilized control.

3.4.1.2   Apparatus and Experimental Design

Directly after fertilization, 15 identical replicate cups with approximately 50 eggs/cup were placed in fertilization trays. The trays were exposed to consistent temperature, constant flow rate, and a programmed light regime consistent with civil sunrise and sunset.. Three days post-fertilization (dpf), five cups were chosen at random and placed in a 75 7-L (20-gal) aquarium centered between Helmholtz coils supplied with a direct current that resulted in a 3-mT EMF equally distributed throughout a 60cm/side cube. This group served as the early EMF-exposed treatment and received constant EMF exposure for 17 days. The remaining cups (including the unfertilized eggs) were moved to an identical aquarium away from the EMF source. At 10 dpf, five cups were chosen at random from the unexposed cups (late EMF-exposed group) and placed in the EMF field alongside the early EMF-exposed group. This produced two groups that received different durations of EMF exposure (17 days and 10 days). This exposure schedule was influenced by a similar study involving zebrafish by Skauli et al (2000). The remaining five cups were left in the unexposed aquarium to serve as a control for exposure, thus resulting in a sample of 5 cups for each exposure group; each cup contained approximately 50 eggs (biological replication).

Daily temperature recordings and frequent flow rate readings were taken in both aquaria to ensure that conditions remained the same. At 20 dpf, the EMF coils were turned off, and each cup was subdivided into two groups. One-half was collected and fixed in Stockard's solution for observation directly following termination of EMF exposure. The other half was allowed to develop until hatching in the absence of the EMF. Twice a day, eggs were observed for newly hatched larvae (fry), which were then removed, documented, and fixed for observation.

3.4.1.3   Post-Mortem and Developmental Progress Scoring

Fertilized 20-dpf eggs were evaluated for the following anatomical indicators of development: straightness of the spinal cord, development of a distinct bi-hemispherical brain, and large dark pigmented eyes. Embryos free of mutations or developmental delays were given a value of 1 for each indicator analyzed, while those embryos with mutations such as scoliosis, eye malformations, and improper brain development were given a 0 for that indicator. At 36 dpf, the remaining embryos and fry collected on or before 36 dpf were scored based on anatomical indicators specific to later developmental stages. These include the following indicators: complete hatching, complete separation of caudal fin from the yolk, opening of the mouth, and straightness of the spine. As described for the 20 dpf embryos, all deformities were given a value of 0, while normal anatomy was given a value of 1. The developmental score for an individual embryo or fry was calculated as the sum of the analyzed parameters; 0 was the smallest possible score (all parameters mutated or delayed), and 3 (20 dpf) or 4 (36 dpf) were the greatest (no mutations or delays). The replicate score was calculated as the average of the individual developmental scores (± standard error, S.E.). All unfertilized eggs were counted, removed, and discarded. Embryo mortalities were removed upon visible signs of death and were tracked by date and exposure group. The mortalities were fixed in Stockard's solution for later observation. In trout, it is typical for as many as 98–99% of embryos reaching the eye stage of development (~28 dpf) to be considered normal, with no obvious malformations (Devaux et al. 2011). However, for some developmental milestones such as eye pigmentation, as many as 20—25% of control embryos may exhibit a delay of up to several days to achieve this milestone (Schultz et al. 2008).

3.4.1.4   Statistical Analysis

For the rainbow trout experiments, a nonparametric Kruskal–Wallis test was used to determine if the median developmental score was significantly different between treatments. Common and separate two-parameter logistic curves were fit to the hatch data. A power analysis was conducted to determine the achieved power for the observed difference between the control and test treatments and an estimated number of replicates required to achieve 80% power. An F-test was used to determine if the separate models were significantly different from a common model for all treatments.

3.4.2   Results

3.4.2.1   Fertilization Success

Fertilization success was used as the endpoint to evaluate how EMF exposure affected overall larval development. Fertilization success was expressed as the percentage of eggs that underwent any embryonic growth (determined at 20 dpf) relative to the total eggs that were fertilized. The unexposed group, the early EMF-exposed group, and the late EMF-exposed groups had fertility successes of 59.8%, 65.4%, and 65.4%, respectively. This level of fertilization success is within the normal range observed in previous studies (Schultz et al. 2003; Brown et al. 2007).

3.4.2.2   Developmental Progress to 20 Days Post-Fertilization

To track developmental progress before hatching, half of the embryos in each cup were removed at 20 dpf and evaluated for their developmental progress; a score of 3 indicated normal development (see

Section 3.4.1 for details on embryo scoring). Embryos observed to be less developed or exhibiting some abnormality had a lower score, depending on the severity. If all embryos for a given replicate were developed normally, then an average sum of the indicator values would result in a score of 3. The average developmental scores for the unexposed control, early exposed, and late exposed groups were 2.98 (±0.01), 3 (±0.00), and 2.83 (±0.04), respectively (Table 3.1). The mean percentages of embryos determined to be normally developed (developmental score equal to 3) were:

- 98.4% (±1.9) for the control group, with two embryos displaying eye malformations

- 100.0% (±0.00) for the early EMF-exposed group, with no embryos showing developmental defects

- 82.0% (±9.6) for the late EMF-exposed group, with embryos showing eye malformations and of those embryos showing brain malformations.

A significantly lower developmental score was observed for the late exposure treatment (p = 0.03). These data suggest that various developmental processes during embryogenesis may be affected by temporal exposures to EMF. Given that eggs were removed from EMF exposure at 20 dpf, it is uncertain if the developmental defects noted would have persisted throughout the remainder of embryogenesis, thereby altering hatching success and fish survival. The achieved statistical power with 5 replicates was estimated to be 2.8%. However, the maximum difference in the developmental score between the control and treatment exposures was extremely small (0.15), suggesting that no EMF effects would be observed at a lower treatment level. The power analysis estimated that 15 replicates per treatment would be needed to be able to detect this level of difference (0.15) at 80% power.

Table 3.1. Summary of 20 dpf Rainbow Trout Embryo Development Scores. Scoring ranged from 0 to 3; 3 was considered normal.

20 dpf	Average developmental score (±S.E.)	Embryos with a score of 3 (%)	Number of embryos with malformations/total number of embryos examined
Unexposed	2.98 (±0.01)	98.4 (±1.9)	2/123
Early exposed	3.00 (±0.00)	100.0 (±0.00)	0/108
Late exposed	2.83 (±0.04)	82.0 (±9.6)	23/128

3.4.2.3 Hatching Rates

Hatching rates across all experimental groups were also examined. The date, time, and number of total fry hatchings per day were recorded for all the treatments (Figure 3.2). The average number of days post-fertilization until hatching for each treatment was as follows:

- 30.6 dpf for the unexposed group (range 24–34 dpf)

- 31 dpf for the early EMF-exposed group (range 25–36 dpf)

- 30 dpf for the late EMF-exposed group (range 25–36 dpf).

A two-parameter logistic curve fit to the data was not significantly different between treatments (p = 0.53), suggesting that EMF-exposure during embryogenesis did not overtly affect the timing of fry emerging from their eggs. The hatching success of the fertilized eggs was 93.7% for the unexposed group (8 embryos did not hatch), 95.6% for the early EMF-exposed group (4 embryos did not hatch), and 98.2% for the late EMF-exposed group (2 embryos did not hatch; Table 3.2).

Table 3.2. Summary of 36 dpf rainbow Trout Fry Hatching Success and Developmental Scores. Scoring ranged from 0 to 4; 4 was considered normal.

36 dpf	Hatching success	Average developmental score (±S.E.)	Embryos with a score of 4 (%)	Number of embryos with malformations/total number of embryos examined
Unexposed	93.7%	3.41 (±0.08)	59.9 (±5.5)	51/127
Early exposed	95.6%	3.51 (±0.13)	65.6 (±9.8)	31/90
Late exposed	98.2%	3.41 (±0.06)	54.3 (±4.4)	54/112

3.4.2.4   Developmental Progress to 36 Days Post-Fertilization

As indicated by Figure 3.2, the majority of embryos in all three groups had hatched by 36 dpf. Examination of developmental markers at 36 dpf provided an indication of whether short-duration EMF exposure during embryogenesis affected overall embryo development (Table 3.2). Although almost all embryos had hatched, transitioning into the fry stage, a few embryos remained in their chorion and were included in the analysis as potential developmentally delayed or deformed specimens. To streamline the reporting, all specimens analyzed at 36 dpf, whether embryo or fry, are referred to as "fry." The average developmental scores ranging from 0 to 4 (4 being developed normally) of the fry for the unexposed group and the early and late EMF-exposed group were 3.41 (±0.08), 3.51 (±0.13), and 3.41 (±0.06), respectively. These scores were not significantly different from each other ($p = 0.88$). The percentage of fry receiving a score indicative of normal development was 59.9% (±5.5%) for the control group; 51 control embryos showed signs of developmental delay or anatomical abnormalities. Of the early EMF-exposed group, 65.6% (±9.8%) were found to have developed normally; 31 embryos in this group showed signs of developmental delay or abnormalities. Of the late EMF-exposed group, 54.3% (±4.4%) developed normally; 54 embryos showed signs of developmental delay or defects.

The statistical power achieved with 5 replicates was estimated to be 7.9%. However, the maximum difference in the developmental score between the control and treatment exposures was extremely small (0.095), which suggests it would be unlikely that EMF effects would be observed at a lower treatment level. The power analysis estimated that more than 103 replicates per treatment would be needed to be able to detect this level of difference (0.095) at 80% power.

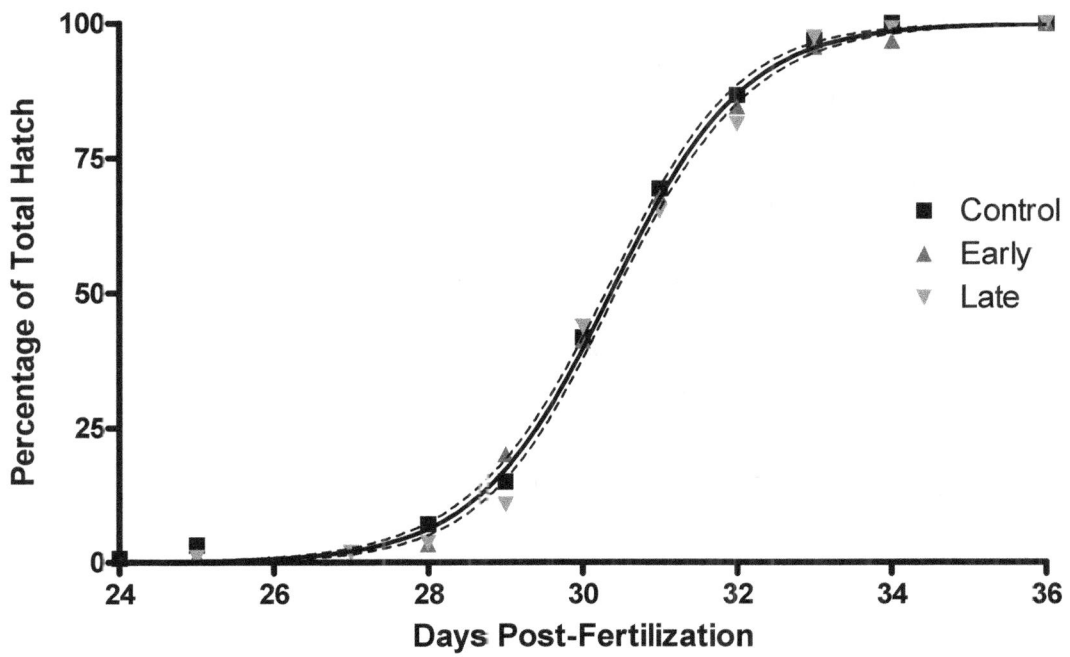

Figure 3.2. Timing for Rainbow Trout Fry Hatching

These results suggest short-duration EMF exposure followed by no EMF exposure does not significantly affect embryogenesis compared to unexposed control embryos. Compared to the significantly lower developmental score noted for the late EMF-exposed group analyzed at 20 dpf, the reprieve from EMF exposure might provide the opportunity for embryo developmental processes to overcome any delay that might occur due to the EMF exposure.

The increase in developmental defects that was noted for the 36 dpf fry over all groups in comparison to the embryos analyzed at 20 dpf could be the result of analyzing different developmental processes at staggered times throughout the process. For example, the mouth opening and the tail detaching from the yolk are late developmental markers, whereas eye pigmentation and bi-hemispherical brain development are early developmental indicators. Because not all embryos develop at the same rate, the additional 16 days would allow for developmental delays to become more prominent when late developmental markers are analyzed. In addition, 36 dpf embryos might display more defects due to the increased stress of handling and separating the embryos at 20 dpf than the embryos harvested at 20 dpf due to the added developmental time. Because of these factors, an increased rate of delay or deformities would be more prominent in later-staged larvae.

3.5 Atlantic Halibut Development and Survival

Atlantic halibut are an important commercial and recreational resource in the North and Mid-Atlantic regions and are under consideration as a species of interest for net-pen and fish farming in Nova Scotia. Larval halibut are found in the water column during early development; then become associated with benthic environments at the completion of the eye migration stage of development. Because the developmental stages of this species have been well characterized (Gisbert et al. 2002; Saele et al. 2004), this species is a good model organism for use in EMF testing. Given their position in the water-column, both larval and adult halibut could receive an exposure from MHK devices and cables. Proper eye migration is closely linked to larval survivorship. If significant developmental effects occur (e.g., delayed or incomplete eye migration or reduced growth), community and population-level effects could conceivably occur.

An exploratory exposure of larval Atlantic Halibut was used to determine if an elevated EMF could affect the developmental phase of marine fish larval–juvenile transformations. Larval Atlantic halibut were exposed to a constant 3-mT EMF field during two distinct periods before metamorphosis to the juvenile stage. This transition is an important stage in halibut development because population recruitment is based on transitioning between larval forms with eyes on both sides of the body to juvenile forms with eyes on one side of the body (Saele et al. 2004). Halibut larvae do not feed for approximately 30 days post-hatch. Thus, researchers often express the age or developmental stage of the larvae as *days post-first feed* (dpff), indicating the days after the halibut larvae begin to accept laboratory food supplements, as described in Section 3.5.1.

3.5.1   Methods

3.5.1.1   Arrival, Care, and Holding

The Atlantic halibut larvae were cultivated and hatched offsite by Scotian Halibut Limited in Halifax, Nova Scotia, Canada. Approximately 1,000 Atlantic halibut larvae aged 22 days dpff arrived at the MSL with an approximate mortality rate of 40%. The fish were fed SELCO-enriched second instar brine shrimp twice a day for the duration of the study. Upon arrival, the halibut were initially held in large cylindrical 300-L tanks with constant filtered seawater flow-through. Tanks were greened with gray porcelain potter's clay following feedings to decrease fish stress. Dead fish and detritus were siphoned from the tanks three times a week, and mortality rates were documented.

3.5.1.2   Apparatus and Experimental Design

Fish were exposed to a 3-mT EMF in two separate experiments: 1) for 32 days starting at 27 days dpff and 2) for 7 days starting at 59 dpff. For Experiment 1, 150 24 dpff larvae were placed in two experimental cubes sized 60 cm on a side and filled with 40 to 50 L of filtered seawater resupplied via a flow-through system. Temperatures were maintained between 9°C and 10°C, and water flow rates ranged between 1 and 2 L/min. The flow rates were adjusted to alter temperature if the cube temperatures differed by more than 0.2°C from each other. One cube was situated directly in the center of the same Helmholtz coils used for the rainbow trout egg exposure, and one cube was set up as the early-established control. Mortalities were counted and removed 2 days after transfer to the cubes. To replace the fish lost, approximately 80 fish were transferred to both the experimental and the control cubes. After 72 hr acclimatization (relative to the initial transfer of 150 larvae), the Helmholtz coil was turned on to produce a 3-mT EMF. At this time, we also established a second control cube (late control) containing 100 larvae at a similar age (27 dpff). After 32 days of EMF exposure, each fish was immediately euthanized by MS-222 overdose and analyzed for the following parameters: degree of eye migration, pigmentation patterning, myotome height, standard length (head to fork), and overall developmental stage.

In Experiment 2, 22 to 24 larvae aged 59 dpff were placed in the EMF and control exposure cubes and exposed to a 3-mT EMF until 63 dpff. At this point, the larvae were transferred to fiberglass culturing tanks until 90 dpff, when they were similarly evaluated as in Experiment 1.

3.5.1.3   Staging of Larvae

In examining developmental progress (staging) of the fish, we gave numerical rankings for pigmentation, eye migration, and overall developmental stage (Table 3.3). Developmental stage was based on both overall size of the fish and the degree of eye migration according to staging data in Saele et al. (2004).

Table 3.3. Pigmentation and Eye Migration Ranking Descriptions

Pigmentation		Eye Migration	
Rank	Description	Rank	Description
1	Unpigmented	0	Eyes symmetrical
2	Ambicolored	1	Half of migrating eye visible
3	Pseudoalbinic	2	Migrating eye is over opposite side, cornea visible, lens is not
4	Asymmetrical	3	Migrating eye on dorsal midline
		4	Migrating eye between final position and dorsal midline
		5	Complete eye migration

3.5.1.4   Statistical Analysis

As an exploratory test, there was no treatment replication for this exposure and therefore no power analysis was conducted. Confidence intervals of 95% were applied to compare the distributions of individual data sets, using Microsoft Excel.

3.5.2   Results

3.5.2.1   Observations of Early and Late Established Control Comparison in Experiment 1

The important difference between the early and late controls is the acclimation time in the exposure cubes prior to the start of the experiment. Two control cubes were established to provide some replication for assessing tank-level variation in larvae growth and development. In order to draw conclusions from a comparison of the EMF-exposed fish with one or both of the control tanks, there must be no variation between the two controls. Important factors that might affect the developmental rates of the early- and late-established controls are starting population density in the cubes and the age of the fish when they were transferred to the cubes. The developmental pigmentation changes were constant across all but one of the 104 fish observed from all three experimental cubes. However, average eye migration stage, average myotome height, average standard length, and the percentage of fish in each developmental stage were different between the early- and late-established controls. The average myotome lengths for the early- and the late-established controls were 3.77 mm (±0.74) and 4.35 mm (±0.13), respectively. The overall fish lengths in the early- and late-established controls were 17.51 mm (±0.22) and 18.37 mm (±0.28), respectively. Because the early- and late-established controls were separate controls, comparisons were made only between the early-established control tank and the EMF-exposed tank established at the same time.

3.5.2.2 Fish Size

Overall fish size was evaluated by measuring myotome height, standard length, and the ratio of the two measurements to determine if EMF affected larval size. There is a comparable relationship between age and size that can represent developmental progress (Saele et al. 2004).

Summary results (average and standard error) for Experiment 1 are presented in Figure 3.3. In Experiment 1, the average myotome height for the early established control and the EMF-exposed treatments were 3.77 mm (±0.12) and 3.73 mm (±0.12), respectively. The average standard length for the early-established control and the EMF-exposed treatments were 17.51 mm (±0.22) and 16.77 mm (±0.22), respectively. The ratio of myotome length to standard length for the early-established control and the EMF-exposed treatments were 0.22 (±0.03) and 0.21 (±0.03), respectively. Larval developmental stages were also subjectively scored based on representative fish diagrams in Saele et al. (2004). Fish stages ranged from 1 to 9 based on cranial ossification, which corresponds highly with eye migration. Stage 9 larvae are defined as having fully completed eye migration. The developmental stage for the early established control group was 7.26 (±0.14) and 7.19 (±0.12) for the EMF-exposed group. The 95% confidence interval of the standard length means are 17.1 to 18.0 for the control and 16.3 and 17.2 for the EMF exposed treatment. The differences between the control tank and EMF-exposed tank for all observed parameters lie within a 95% confidence interval of one another and thus were not considered to be statistically different.

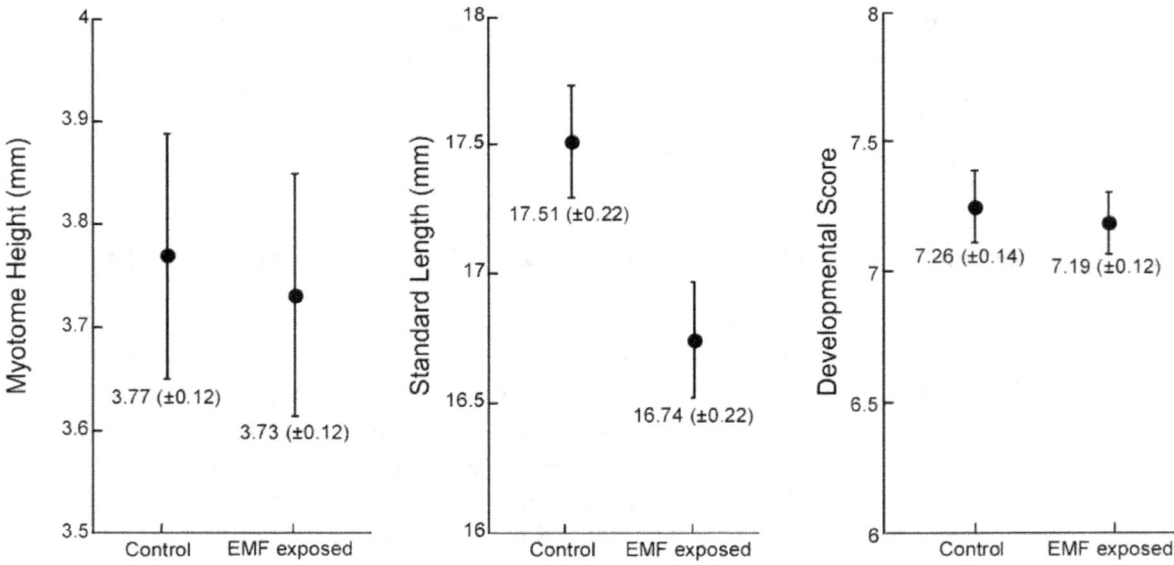

Figure 3.3. Comparison of Average (±S.E.) Measurement for Myotome Height, Standard Length, and Developmental Score

3.5.2.3 Mortality Rate

The average mortality rate in each cube was calculated by counting and removing dead fish three times a week. Based on the slope of best fit for the population numbers per tank, an average mortality rate was calculated to be 2.98%/day for the early-established control and 3.03%/day for the EMF-exposed tank (Figure 3.4). An exponential decay model with a common plateau can be fit to both curves ($R^2 > 0.95$). However, the decay rates were significantly different (p = 0.003). At the time of termination, only 21.5% of the early-established cube and 23.1% of the EMF-exposed cube were still alive. This high degree of mortality is not unexpected with larval flatfish, and losses of 80% have been frequently reported.

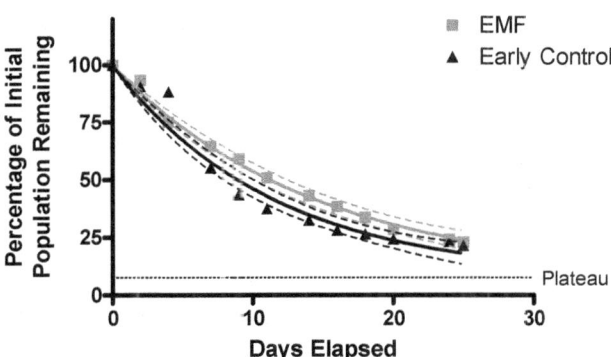

Figure 3.4. Mortality Rate of Atlantic Halibut in Each Experimental Cube Shown as EMF-Exposed (EMF) Data and Early-Established Control (Early Control) Data. The expected regression curve and 95% confidence interval are plotted for each dataset.

In Experiment 2, we examined the same developmental parameters as in Experiment 1. The average myotome heights for the control and EMF-exposed treatments were 7.12 mm (±0.30) and 5.74 mm (±0.25), respectively. The average standard lengths for the early-established control and the EMF-exposed treatments were 24.5 mm (±0.8) and 20.5 mm (±0.7), respectively. Subjective comparison of larval staging found that the majority of EMF-exposed larvae were in larval stage 8 compared to the control fish where the majority had completed metamorphosis (Figure 3.5). However, the differences between the control tank and EMF-exposed tank with respect to these parameters were within a 95% confidence interval and thus were not considered to be statistically different. In this experiment, overall mortality was low, with more than 90% survival of the control and EMF fish. Although these two experimental studies are preliminary and require repeating to confirm the findings, the overall trends noted suggest that Atlantic halibut larvae-to-juvenile morphogenesis is not overtly affected by EMF.

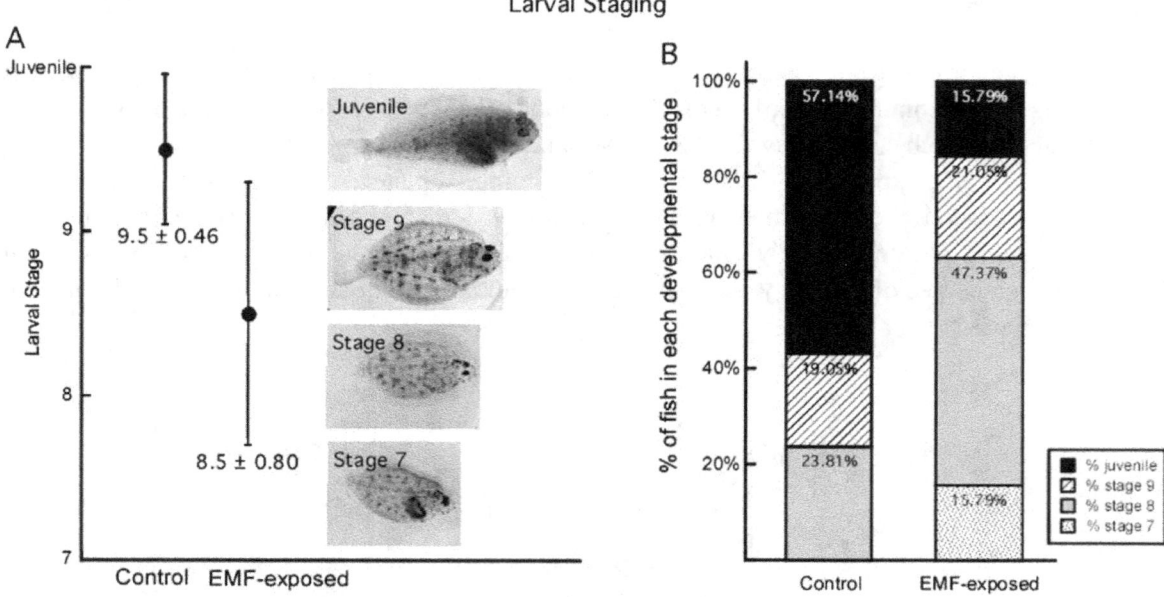

Figure 3.5. Staging of Halibut Larvae at 90 Days Post-First Feed. A) Larvae received a score of 0 to juvenile; juvenile fish had completed eye migration. The average (± 95% confidence interval) is presented with corresponding images from each developmental stage. B) Distribution percentage of larvae in each treatment group, ranging from developmental stage 7 to juvenile stage.

3.6 California Halibut Growth and Development

California halibut were also used as a model flatfish to evaluate the effect of EMF exposure on the larval–juvenile transformation. California halibut were received from The Cultured Abalone, Ltd. (Santa Barbara, California) at the Marine Sciences Laboratory within 72 hr of hatching. Through preliminary culturing efforts, we developed a protocol that maximized fish survivability and permitted testing during the period when metamorphosis is occurring. Using this new protocol, 48 hr post-hatch larvae were cultured to 32 days post-hatch, when most larvae were in the flexion–postflexion developmental stage and close to the initiation of eye migration. At this point, the larvae were used in experiments described in the following subsections.

3.6.1 Methods

California halibut were contained in two 9.5-L (2.5-gal) aquaria nested in large water baths (Figure 2.3). Larval staging was examined prior to the start of exposure, and each tank received equal numbers of each stage totaling 18–20 fish per tank. Two tanks were situated directly in the center of the Helmholtz coils, and two tanks were placed outside the coil influence and used as control replicates. EMF-exposed larvae were subjected to DC EMF at 3 mT. Larvae were held in their respective treatment tanks until all larvae in the control tanks had completed metamorphosis, which occurred 12 days after the exposure began. After the experiment ended, each fish was measured for standard length, eye migration stage, pigmentation pattern, and developmental stage. A nonparametric Kruskal–Wallis test was used to determine if the median developmental score was significantly different between treatments. A chi-square test was used to compare the number of larvae in each stage for a given treatment. A power analysis was also conducted to determine the achieved power for the observed difference between the control and test treatments and an estimated number of replicates required to achieve 80% power.

3.6.2   Results

Survival of the larvae during the exposure was 63–74% for the control group and 42–47% for the EMF-exposed groups. Indices of metamorphosis such as standard (fork) length (8.29mm ±0.19 for the control and 8.66mm ±0.56 for the EMF-exposed group) and eye migration stage (2.18 ±0.03 for the control and 2.18 ±0.07 for the EMF-exposed group) were similar between both treatment groups (Table 3.4), as was the average stage of larval development (8.14 ±0.28 for the control group and 7.83 ±0.05 for the EMF-exposed group). None of the parameters analyzed were significantly different (p > 0.439). In addition, the number of larvae per stage of development was compared between the control and EMF-exposed groups, but no significant differences were observed (p = 0.332).

The achieved statistical powers for standard length, eye migration, and average developmental scores with 2 replicates were estimated to be 6.8%, 5%, and 10% respectively. However, the maximum differences in these parameters between the control and treatment exposures were 0.59 mm in length, 0.08 in eye migration score, and 0.31 in developmental score, which suggests that responses to EMF would not be observed at a lower intensity. The power analysis estimated that 35, 11, and 9 replicates per treatment would be needed to be able to detect a difference of 5% in these parameters, respectively, at 80% power.

Table 3.4. Summary of California Halibut Development After 12 Days at 3-mT Exposure

	Std. Length in mm, mean (S.E.)	Eye Migration, mean (S.E.)	Average Stage, mean (S.E.)
Control	8.29 (±0.19)	2.18 (±0.03)	8.14 (±0.28)
EMF-exposed	8.66 (±0.56)	2.18 (±0.07)	7.83 (±0.05)

3.7   Summary of FY 2010 and FY 2011 Fish Experiments

During FY 2010 and FY 2011, a variety of experiments were conducted with ecologically, commercially, and recreationally important fish species to determine if exposure to EMF from MHK devices and cables would have an adverse measureable effect at the specie level. The results of these studies are summarized in Table 3.5. Behavioral experiments with coho salmon were inconclusive, due primarily to non-treatment influences that masked a potential behavioral response to EMF. There was, however, no compelling evidence that exposure to EMF affected the ability of this species to detect predators. Exposure marker experiments showed no evidence of stress (exhibited as cortisol production) while exposed to EMF; however, some evidence was seen of reduced melatonin levels after exposure to EMF although it was not statistically significant. Exposure of fertilized trout eggs to 3-mT EMF for extended periods appeared to influence egg development but was also not statistically significant. Experiments with Atlantic halibut suggested exposure to 3-mT EMF reduced both growth and development, but neither endpoint was statistically different from the control; changes to growth and development of California halibut were not observed.

Although EMF experimental exposures approaching 3 mT have appeared in peer-reviewed literature, this field strength may be higher than that occurring near MHK devices or from cables associated with the devices, based on several recent reports. For example, recent reports of measured EMF levels associated with underwater power cables emanating from off-shore wind farms suggest peak exposures are in the range of 0.4 to 1.6 µT (CMACS 2003; Gill et al. 2009). Assuming field intensity is an important EMF characteristic, a 3 mT EMF exposure level then provides a safety margin to account for some limitations of laboratory testing such as statistical power. Most of the exposures conducted at 3 mT did not result in statistically significant changes to survival, growth, or development in the species tested in FY 2010 and FY 2011. However, the statistical power of some tests was affected by the physical constraints imposed by the Helmholtz test system (e.g., finite number of exposure containers that could be tested at a given time), or test organism availability or life-history traits that affected test design (e.g., larval fish availability). In addition, one exposure marker, melatonin, did show a decrease in levels as a response to an elevated EMF exposure. However, the overall effect and biological significance of decreased melatonin on whole-animal behavior has not been assessed.

Table 3.5. Summary of EMF Experiments with Fish from FY 2010 and FY 2011

Experiment	Species Tested	Testing Endpoint	Result
Coho salmon alarm response	Coho salmon (*O. kisutch*)	Decreased swimming	Inconclusive. All fish appeared to be highly stressed in exposure cubes w/wo EMF & unresponsive to alarm substance
Coho salmon exposure marker	Coho salmon (*O. kisutch*)	Melatonin/cortisol	Decreased melatonin levels in 3 mT and 0.13 mT (AC) treatments, not statistically significant
Trout egg development	Rainbow trout (*O. mykiss*)	Survival and development	Short-duration EMF exposure caused apparent developmental delay at 20 dpf
Atlantic halibut effects	Atlantic Halibut (*H. hippoglossus*)	Growth	EMF-exposed larvae were slightly smaller, not statistically significantly
		Development	EMF exposure slightly delayed larval development, not statistically significant
California halibut effects	California Halibut (*P. californicus*)	Growth	No effect
		Development	No effect

3.8   FY 2012 Activities

FY 2012 activities will include exposure assessments of a representative elasmobranch (e.g. shark, skate, or ray). We are currently assessing the options with respect to relevance, availability, ease of handling, and stage of life and organism size. In addition, the Helmholtz coil will be reconfigured if necessary to accommodate the nature and size of the species selected. Previously conducted fish exposures and available literature will be used to guide the experimental design.

4.0 Invertebrate Experiments

4.1 Introduction

Dungeness crab (*Metacarcinus magister*) are an ecologically, commercially, and recreationally important resource in temperate coastal ecosystems ranging between Alaska and California. Because there is anecdotal evidence that some species of crustaceans may be sensitive to EMF, a series of exploratory experiments were conducted to 1) evaluate crab sensitivity to EMF, 2) assess the influence of EMF on the ability to detect food, and 3) evaluate whether the presence of EMF from electrical cables caused an avoidance or attraction response. Antennular flicking rate was used as an endpoint for EMF detection and food detection experiments; crab position and behavior (burying or visible on sediment surface) in relation to EMF was used to support avoidance/attraction exposures. A large body of literature supports the use of antennular flicking rate as a chemosensory measure for detecting food, pheromones, and predators; other stimuli such as vibration and sound also are known to elicit a flicking response. However, the use of this endpoint to assess an EMF increase or detection of a food extract in the presence of EMF has not been previously tested.

Tests were conducted using the Helmholtz coil system described in Section 2; sensitivity and food detection experiments were conducted at approximately 3 mT (DC). To support avoidance/attraction experiments, the coils were reconfigured to create a decaying field emanating from the center of a rectangular enclosure at approximately 1 mT (DC). For all experiments, a combination of visual observations and video recordings was used to document endpoints of interest.

4.1.1 Testing Goals and Objectives

The testing goals for Dungeness crab for FY 2011 were focused on behavioral endpoints that could be measured in the laboratory and would provide a range of assessment criteria:

- *Phase 1 – Detection of acute EMF exposure* – Determine the ability of Dungeness crab to detect an acute increase in an upper bounding level of EMF (3 mT DC) using antennular flicking rate as a measurable endpoint response.

- *Phase 2 – Detection of a food odor in the presence of EMF* – Determine the ability of Dungeness crab to detect the presence of a food odor (clam extract) after a moderate-duration exposure (~20 hr) to 3 mT DC EMF.

- *Phase 3 – Avoidance/attraction to EMF* – Develop a protocol and assess the behavioral response of crab when presented with choices of location in a spatially decaying EMF field.

4.1.2 Test Organism and Holding Facilities

Locally trapped adult male Dungeness crabs (*M. carcinus*) were used for all test exposures. Crabs were held at the MSL in outdoor tanks containing approximately 20 cm (~8 in.) of clean sand and unfiltered flow-through seawater from Sequim Bay. They were held for 1 to 3 weeks until tested, and crabs were provided an ad libitum diet of native bivalves or fish. When testing occurred, crabs were moved to the indoor experimental system and food was withheld for the duration of testing.

4.2 Detection of Acute EMF Exposure

The initial phase of experimentation with Dungeness crab was conducted in fall 2010 to determine, in a broad sense, whether a crab's response to an acute increase in EMF exposure was overtly obvious, subtle, or nonexistent. The results of these experiments, based on the antennular flicking rate and other behavioral movements as a proxy for detection, were then used to design follow-on tests.

4.2.1 Experimental Design

For the Phase 1 experiments—detection of EMF—the exposure system shown in Figure 2.7 was used. The test system contained four plastic chambers (30 cm × 20 cm × 20 cm); each chamber was fitted with an opaque plexiglass cover clamped to it. A funnel and inlet manifold delivered approximately 1 L/min of 35-μ filtered flow-through seawater from a dripper arm to the bottom of each chamber. A photoperiod synchronized to civil sunrise and sunset provided approximately 500 lux of daylight spectrum lighting.

Four crabs were moved from outdoor holding tanks to the testing system and allowed to acclimate overnight before testing. Seawater flow rates were adjusted, and partitions were placed completely around the testing apparatus to reduce visual disturbance to the crab, both prior to and during testing. Small openings in the partition allowed for camera placement and video recording as well as visual observation (Figure 2.8). Each day of testing occurred entirely within an incoming or outgoing tidal cycle during daylight hours.

For each test, the initial position and posture of each crab was noted (e.g., anterior or posterior placement, resting, standing, antennules active or retracted). To initiate testing, the video recorder was turned on to record images from four cameras simultaneously, capturing the crab's body posture, movement, and antennular flicking rate of one antennule (Figure 4.1). In addition, a trained observer recorded the flicking rate of one crab for the duration of the test as a quality assurance measure. The crab's behavior was recorded for 5 min (i.e., EMF off); the Helmholtz coil was then turned on, generating 3 mT EMF DC, and the recording continued for an additional 5 min (i.e., EMF on).

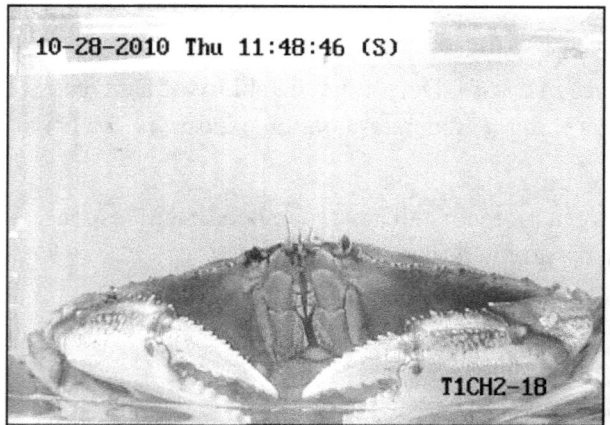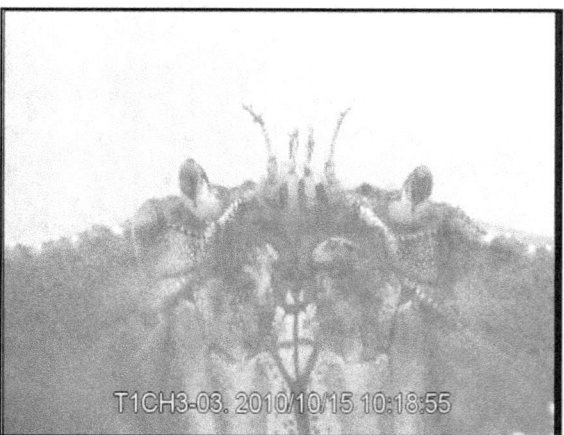

Figure 4.1. Video Images of a Dungeness Crab in the EMF Exposure Chamber in a Resting Position (left) and a Close-Up of the Antennules Centered Between the Antenna and Eyestalk (right)

The video data for each crab was post-processed, and antennular flicking rate per minute was measured for the 5 min prior to and 5 min during the EMF exposure. A one-sample *t*-test was used to test the null hypothesis that the difference between the average pre- and average post-exposure antennular flicking rate was equal to zero. Additional behavioral observations were also evaluated to assess the response to an acute exposure to EMF.

A combined statistical power analysis was conducted for all flicking rate experiments (i.e., detection of EMF, detection of food cue during EMF exposure) to determine if the number of replicates tested achieved 80% power for a range of detectable differences. A difference of 10 flicks/min was used as a standard for comparison. The results of the power analysis for all flicking rate experiments is presented in Section 4.5.

4.2.2   Results

Observations of 34 crabs were evaluated by post-processing the video recordings prior to and during an acute EMF exposure. Eleven crabs were removed from this analysis because some minute intervals were missing (e.g., antennules retracted, not visible to camera). Therefore, twenty-three crabs were evaluated as a time series of the number of flicks per minute; five 1-min intervals were evaluated before EMF exposure (i.e., minute 1 through 5) followed by five 1-min intervals during exposure to EMF (i.e., minute 6 through 10).

The range of pre-EMF exposure flicking rate averaged between 5.6 to 40 flicks/min, which was consistent with the flicking rate of a resting Dungeness crab found in Pearson et al. (1979; 5 to 47 flicks/min). The mean pre-exposure flicking rate was 17 ± 3.6 flicks/min. The average flicking rate during EMF exposure was 15.2 ± 2.7 flicks/min. Figure 4.2 shows the mean antennular flicking rate per minute pre-exposure (EMF off) and during a 3 mT exposure (EMF on). Although a slight decrease was noted between the pre-exposure flicking rate of 17/min and during-exposure rate of 15.2/min, a parametric comparison of the difference between the average flicking rate response for each crab pre- (1-5 min) and during-(6-10 min) exposure was not statistically significant (one-sample two-sided *t*-test; $n = 23$; $p = 0.21$).

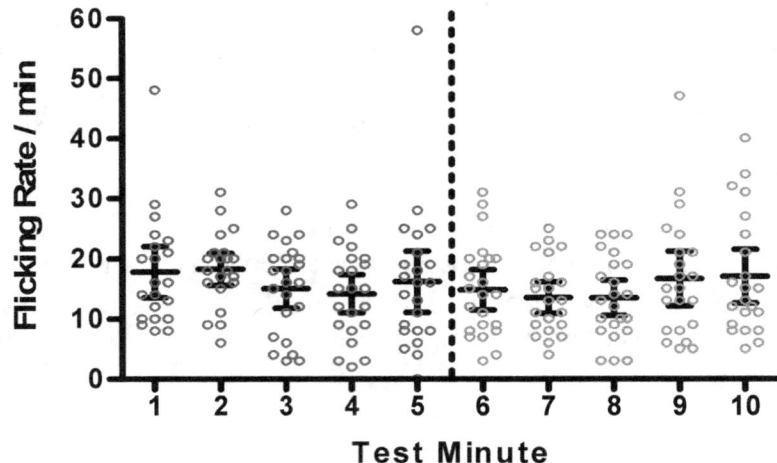

Figure 4.2. Mean (± 95% confidence interval) Dungeness Crab Antennular Flicking Rate ($n = 23$) for 5 min prior to EMF Exposure (blue circles) and 5 min During a 3-mT DC EMF Exposure (red circles).

Video recordings captured additional behavioral responses during the pre-exposure and acute EMF exposure trials, however these were anecdotal to our primary response variable being examined. These changes included the posture in the test chamber prior to testing and during EMF exposure (i.e., resting, sleeping with eyestalks retracted in sockets, standing, and climbing), and other movements associated with the antennae, eyestalks, mouthparts, dactyls, and chelae. To date, these behaviors have not been analyzed quantitatively.

4.3 Food Detection During EMF Exposure

Phase 2 of experimentation evaluated the ability of Dungeness crab to recognize a food odor source after an approximate 20-hr exposure to a 3-mT EMF source. Crabs were exposed to filtered seawater (SW) as a stimulant and/or a food extract (FD) derived from clams. Each experimental trial was conducted with naïve (untested) crabs using a low-dose FD (Trial 1) or high dose FD (Trial 2):

- *Trial 1* – 20-hr exposure to 3-mT DC EMF or control (no exposure), then measured antennular flicking response after presentation of a filtered SW extract (control) <u>or</u> a 10^{-6}-g/L FD (low-dose treatment).

- *Trial 2* – 20-hr exposure to 3-mT DC EMF or control (no exposure), then measured antennular flicking response of each crab to a SW extract (control) <u>followed by</u> a 10^{-1}-g/L FD (high-dose treatment).

4.3.1 Experimental Design

The exposure test system used for Phase 2 experimentation was the same as that used for Phase 1 (Section 4.2.1, Figure 2.7 (left), Figure 2.8) with the exception of the addition of a buret delivery system for adding SW and/or FD (Figure 2.7, right). The day before testing, up to four naïve crabs were transferred to the testing chambers, the seawater flow rate adjusted, and blinds secured. The Helmholtz coils were either turned on to deliver an approximate 20-hr, 3-mT EMF exposure or left off, providing a background EMF exposure (control).

4.3.1.1 Test Procedures

For Trial 1, a total of 44 crabs were tested. Trial 1 replicates consisted of a 20-hr exposure, (i.e. 3-mT DC EMF or background EMF), and a randomly assigned treatment presented at the end but during the exposure (i.e. 20 mL of filtered SW as a control odor stimulus or 10^{-6}-g/L FD clam stimulus) for each crab. The order of testing was assigned randomly. For each crab a 10 minute time series of antennular flicks was video recorded. The initial 5 minutes recorded the response during the end of the 20-hr of EMF exposure (3 mT or background). A randomly assigned SW or FD stimulus was then introduced into the chamber at minute 6 from a buret and tubing connected to the funnel and inlet manifold (Figure 2.7), with video recording continuing for an additional 5 minutes. The video data for each crab were post-processed and evaluated statistically to examine the SW and 10^{-6}-g/L FD treatment responses to background and EMF exposures.

For statistical analyses, individual time series for each crab were characterized by averages over time, differences between periods of time, or responses of a specific minute. A nonparametric Kruskal-Wallis test was used to compare the average of the first 5-min flicking rate between exposures (background and 3-mT EMF), and to compare the four treatment combination medians at minute 6 (EMF-SW, EMF-FD, Background-SW, Background-FD). A general linear model (GLM) was also used to assess the magnitude of differences in effects (EMF exposure and FD treatment) and their interaction. Ninety-five percent confidence intervals were calculated as the mean $\pm t_{(\alpha,n-1)}$·(standard error of the mean) to describe selected time periods.

For Trial 2, a total of 27 crabs were tested. Trial 2 replicates were initiated with a 20-hr exposure (i.e. 3-mT DC EMF or background EMF) as in Trial 1. However, the treatment presented during the end of the exposure consisted of each crab receiving 20 mL of SW followed by 20 mL of a high dose of FD (10^{-1} g/L) stimulant approximately 40 min later. For each crab 2- 10 minute time series of flicking responses were recorded. For the initial 10 minute series, video recorded a 5-min flicking response during the end of the 20-hr exposure (3 mT EMF or background), followed by a SW treatment similar to Trial 1 at minute 6, and recording through minute 10 (i.e. 5 min post-SW treatment). A second 10-minute time series was recorded approximately 40 minutes later; 5 minutes of video were recorded followed by introduction of the high dose of FD (10^{-1} g/L) stimulant, then 5 min post-FD treatment, for a total of 20 min of video observations per crab. The time series for each crab was analyzed as in Trial 1. A Kruskal-Wallis test was used to compare the first 5-min flicking rate between exposures (background and 3-mT EMF) and to compare the treatment combination medians from 1 minute post treatment. A GLM was again used to assess the magnitude of differences in effects (EMF exposure and FD treatment) and their interaction. Ninety-five percent confidence intervals were calculated.

4.3.1.2 Preparation of Treatment Stimulus Extracts

The FD used as an odor stimulant for the crabs was prepared from native littleneck clams (*Protothaca staminea*). Clams were held in outdoor holding tanks long enough to purge sediment. The shucked clam meat and liquid was freeze-dried, powdered, and stored at −80°C (−112°F). For testing, a stock solution was prepared by mixing a weighed portion of the FD powder with 0.45-μ filtered SW. This solution was mixed for approximately 2 hr, then filtered through pre-tared glass fiber pre-filters and Whatman GF/C filters. The final FD stock concentration was corrected for loss of material retained on the filters. A stock solution was used for up to 5 days to create the daily stimulus extract used for testing. For each day of testing, the FD stimulus solution was made shortly before testing using fresh-filtered SW from the experimental test source. An aliquot of the test source water was used as the SW control stimulant. Both stimulants were kept in a water bath at ambient temperature until use, when 20 mL was delivered through burets calibrated to deliver at a specified rate. The effective concentration of FD stimulus delivered to the test chambers was 10^{-6} g/L for Trial 1 (low dose) and 10^{-1} g/L for Trial 2 (high dose).

4.3.2   Results

4.3.2.1   Trial 1 – Low-Dose Stimulant Response

During Trial 1, 44 crabs were tested and evaluated through video post-processing of antennular flicking rate, for EMF-exposed or EMF-background crabs that received either a SW or low-dose FD stimulant. Five 1-min interval recordings of each crab were evaluated prior to introduction of the SW or FD stimulant, and the 1-min interval was evaluated after stimulant introduction. Twenty-one crabs were removed from analysis because of missing data (e.g., antennules retracted, not visible to camera), leaving 23 crabs included in the statistical analysis.

The range of pre-odor stimulus flicking rates was similar between exposure groups and similar to Phase 1 background flicking responses (Figure 4.3a); EMF off (SW) 15.6 ±9.7 flicks/min, EMF on (SW) 16.0 ±6.7, EMF off (low-dose FD) 16.8 ±4.9, EMF on (low-dose FD) 20.8 ±10.6. There was no statistically significant difference between medians from any of these pre-stimulus treatments (Kruskal–Wallis, p = 0.46). The 1-min post-stimulus flicking rates were similar between EMF off (SW) 29.6 ± 12.8, and EMF on (SW) 28.0 ± 15.5, and between EMF off (FD) 49.0 ± 12.4, and EMF on (FD) 46 ± 22.8. There was a statistically significant difference in the median 1-min post-stimulus flicking rates (Kruskal–Wallis, p = 0.034), based on greater flicking rates by crabs presented with FD compared to those receiving SW (GLM; error degrees of freedom (d.f.) = 14; p = 0.005). However, the difference between those exposed to 3-mT EMF and those receiving background EMF was not statistically significant (GLM; error d.f. = 14; p = 0.68).

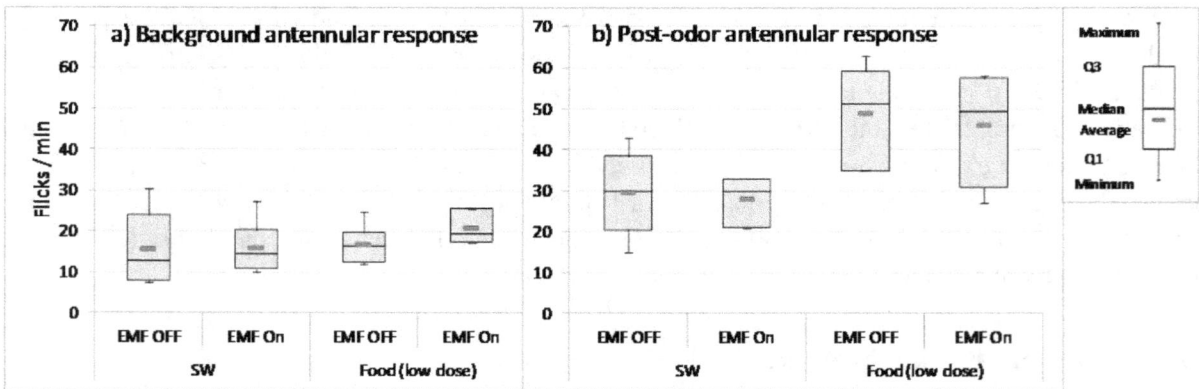

Figure 4.3. Phase 2 – Trial 1 Results of Antennular Flicking Rate. a) Averaged 5 min prior to odor stimulant introduction (seawater [SW] or low-dose 10^{-6}-g/L food extract) of those exposed to background EMF (EMF off) or 3-mT DC (EMF on); b) 1 min after stimulant introduction.

4.3.2.2   Trial 2 – High-Dose Stimulant Response

During Trial 2, the antennular flicking rate of 27 crabs was evaluated; however, a higher dose of FD (10^{-1} g/L) was used. In addition, each crab was tested using SW stimulant initially, followed by a high dose of FD stimulant a short time later. Five 1-min intervals of each crab were evaluated pre-SW or FD stimulant introduction and five 1-min intervals evaluated after stimulant introduction. One crab was removed from analysis because of incomplete data (e.g., antennules retracted, not visible to camera).

The background antennular response flicking rates were similar to those in Phase 1 and Phase 2 – Trial 1 (Figure 4.4a); EMF-off (SW) 18.5 ± 7.5, EMF-on (SW) 14.9 ± 5.2, EMF-off (high-dose FD) 14.7 ± 7.1 and EMF-on (high-dose FD) 11.9 ± 3.9. There was no statistically significant difference between the background flicking rates for SW and FD (Kruskal–Wallis; p = 0.38 and p = 0.45, respectively). In general, for all treatment combinations the 1-min post-stimulus flicking rates (figure 4.4b) were higher than background flicking rates (Figure 4.4 a), with the median differences between pre- and post- greater than eight flicks per minute for all treatment combinations. The one minute post-flicking rates were EMF-off (SW) 29.7 ± 9.6, EMF-on (SW) 21.1 ± 7.0, EMF-off (high-dose FD) 39.0 ± 18.6, EMF-on (high-dose FD) 32.9 ± 13.2). The 1-min post-stimulus flicking rates were not statistically different between the post-SW response for EMF on and off (Kruskal–Wallis, p = 0.14) or the post-FD response for EMF on and off (Kruskal-Wallis, p = 0.30). However, the flicking rates of the EMF-exposed crabs for both stimuli were 11 flicks per minute lower than those of the non-exposed crab (GLM; error d.f. = 41; p = 0.19). Figure 4.4b also shows a higher mean flicking rate of the 1-min post-FD stimulant crabs compared to that of the 1-min post-SW stimulant crabs, regardless of whether the EMF was on or not, although it was not statistically significant (GLM; error d.f. = 41; p = 0.06).

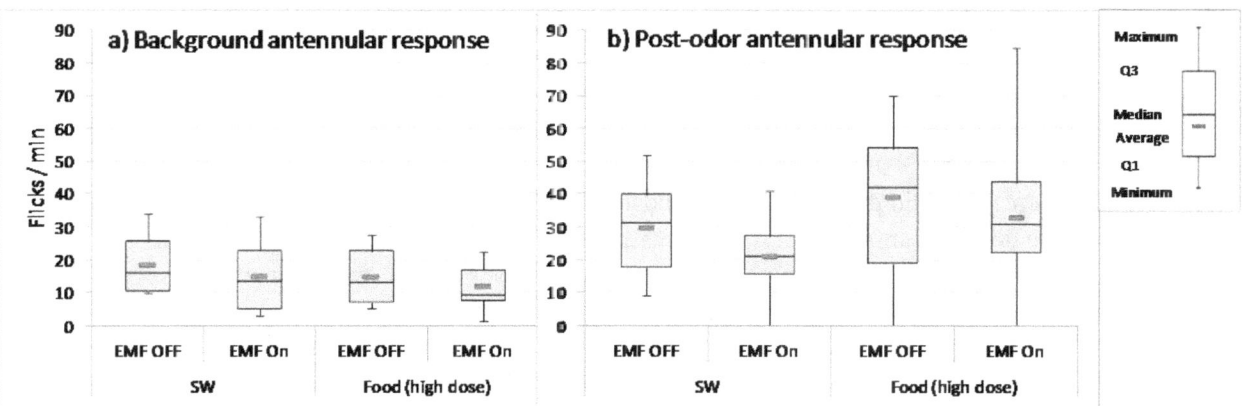

Figure 4.4. Phase 2 – Trial 2 Results of Antennular Flicking Rate. a) Averaged 5 min prior to odor stimulant introduction (seawater [SW] or high-dose 10^{-1}-g/L food stimulant) of those exposed to background EMF (EMF off) or 3 mT DC (EMF on); b) 1 min after stimulant introduction.

Other feeding behaviors were noted in most of the crabs that received the high dose of the FD such as moving from a resting position to standing or dactyl probing. These responses occurred more often with crabs receiving the higher FD dose (10^{-1} g/L) than the lower FD dose (10^{-6} g/L). Crabs that received the higher dose as part of Trial 2 exhibited more active behavior in general than those receiving the lower dose as part of Trial 1. Because of the increased activity level in Trial 2, the antennules were out of view of the camera more frequently. Hence, some of the presumed higher flicking rate counts could not be included in this analysis, and their exclusion may partially explain why the mean flicking rates for the higher dose in Trial 2 were slightly lower than those in Trial 1 with used a lower FD dose. Statistical analysis of other behavioral responses for both Trials 1 and 2 may provide a useful and comparable evaluation between treatments and trial, including dactyl probing, chelae movement, and change in antennular orientation. This may provide additional EMF response data of the crab's ability to detect EMF, or be influenced by EMF with food odor stimulants present.

4.4   Avoidance/Attraction to EMF

4.4.1   Experimental Design

The test system was reconfigured using larger tanks to allow crabs freedom of movement in a decaying EMF, allowing observation of location (EMF zone), and activities within each zone. Two 1700-L (~450-gal) tanks, 3.3 m × 0.75 m × 0.69 m (10.8 ft × 2.5 ft × 2.3 ft) were used as control and exposure, with one coil centered over each tank (Sections 2.1, 2.2.2, Figure 2.8). The coil centered over the exposure tank was energized to provide an average of 1.1 mT DC EMF in the center, decaying approximately an order of magnitude toward each end of the tank (Figure 2.3). The coil centered over the control tank was not energized, with an average background of 0.12 mT DC EMF. Filtered SW [13.9 ± 0.5°C, 30.7 ± 0.8 psu, 6.4 ± 0.2 mg L^{-1} dissolved oxygen, pH 7.4 ± 0.2] entered the tanks at approximately 24 L/min. Subdued daylight spectrum lighting (16 ± 3.5 lux) provided illumination on a photoperiod synchronized to civil sunrise and sunset. Clean sand (15-cm [6-in.] depth) in each tank provided adequate depth for crabs to bury at will. Baffles at either end of the tank allowed a uniform longitudinal flow from one end to the other. The effective surface area of available crab habitat was 2.45 m × 0.75 m (8 ft × 2.5 ft). Video cameras recorded the crabs' behavior for the duration of the experiment, including nighttime using infrared illumination.

4.4.1.1   Test Procedures

Prior to the experiment, 10 untested adult male Dungeness crabs, tagged with unique identifiers on their carapace, were placed in the control and exposure tanks (5 crabs per tank). They were partitioned individually at the downstream end of each tank with a PVC enclosure and allowed to acclimate for 30 min with the coil energized in the exposure tank. Previous experience with this species suggests a 30-min acclimation time was sufficient to mitigate for non-treatment behavioral responses. At the initiation of the experiment, the structures were removed and observations were video recorded for 72 hr. Live observations were made every 30 min during the day, noting the location and behavior of each crab.

4.4.1.2   Video Processing and Statistical Analysis

The video data were analyzed statistically using five zone locations delineated in the exposure tank, based on the EMF strength. Figure 4.5 shows the zone locations, surface area in each zone, and the average EMF intensity, defined for statistical purposes within a zone as the mean ± S.D., recognizing that the EMF intensity decays over a short distance (Figure 2.3). They include Zone 1 – low dose (downstream); Zone 2 – mid-dose (downstream); Zone 3 – high dose (center); Zone 4 – mid-dose (upstream); and Zone 5 – low dose (upstream). The amount of surface area in each zone was determined by the measured EMF; hence, the surface area varied slightly in each zone. For comparison, the zone delineations were replicated in the control tank; background EMF is shown in the bottom half of Figure 4.5. The behavior of each crab was scored at the end of every 15 min and noted as buried, resting on the surface of the sediment (Figure 4.6), or as one of a variety of active behaviors including walking and digging.

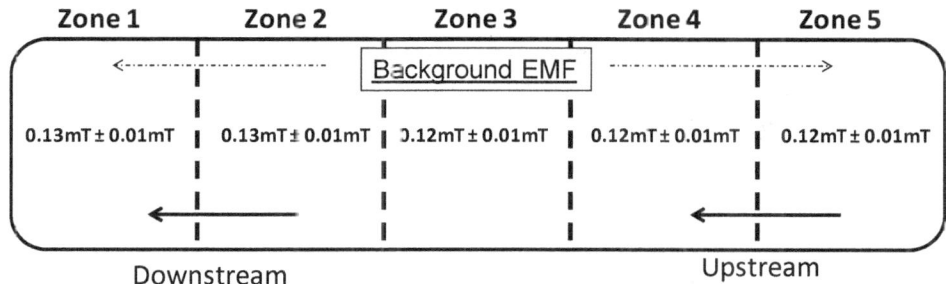

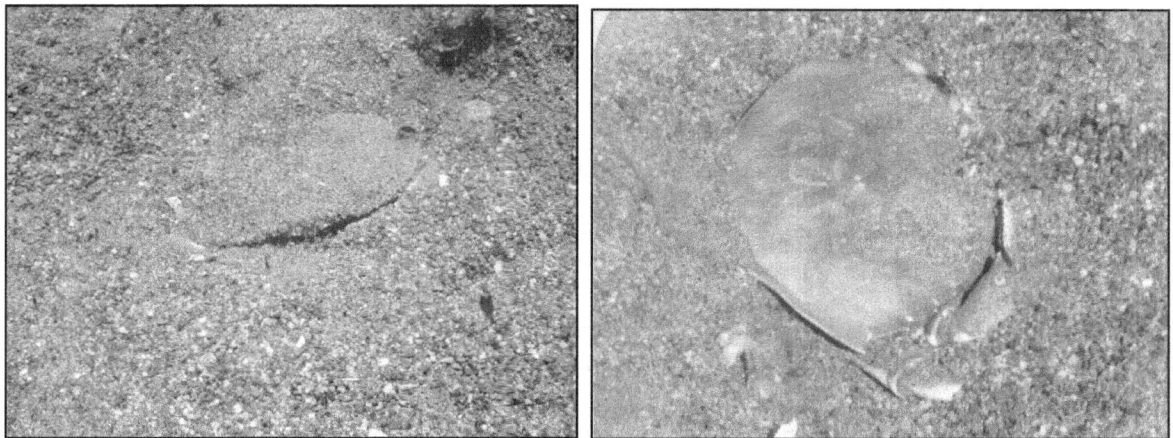

Figure 4.5. EMF Zone Delineations and Surface Area (cm^2) in Experimental Tanks for Avoidance/Attraction Tests. Top, exposure tank; bottom, control tank. EMF intensities (mean ± S.D.) shown within each zone.

Figure 4.6. Examples of Typical Burial Behavior of Crab in Sediment

For the first statistical analysis, behaviors were classified into two categories; buried and active/resting. Because crabs spent on average 83 percent of their time buried, for a specific crab successive 15-min intervals spent buried were not considered independent. Thus, using only those counts of 15-minute intervals when crabs were active or resting, a 2 x 3 chi-square analysis was used to test the null hypothesis that an equal proportion of crabs were observed in each zone (low, mid, and high) between the control and exposure treatment.

The length of time each crab remained buried during testing was independent and calculated for each zone and exposure treatment. The expected number of minutes a crab would remain buried in any zone was calculated based on the proportional area of that zone multiplied by the total number of minutes crabs were observed buried in each exposure treatment. The number of times a crab changed behavior between active, resting, or buried was also calculated. For each of these variables and zones, a nonparametric Kruskal–Wallis test was used to compare EMF exposure treatments. A statistical power analysis was conducted for the avoidance/attraction experiments to determine if the number of crab tested was adequate to achieve 80% power if a difference of 10 activity changes occurred on any given day of testing.

4.4.2 Results

During the 3-day experiment, 2890 observations taken at 15-min intervals were made on the locations and activities of 10 crabs. Six observations were made while the crabs were moving between EMF zones and were removed from further analysis. Initial analysis of the data focused on two behavioral endpoints—the zone location of the crab in relation to the electromagnetic field (low, moderate, high) and whether or not they were buried. Table 4.1 shows the number of crab observations for the duration of the experiment based on zone location and activity level. The proportion of observations of the active or resting crabs in each of the zones was not significantly different between the control and EMF-exposed crabs (chi-square, $p = 0.32$).

The average number of minutes crabs were buried in each tank was examined in each zone. In the low EMF zone, the control crabs remained buried significantly longer than the EMF exposed crabs (Kruskal–Wallis, $p = 0.016$). The observed number of minutes that crabs spent time in the low EMF zone were significantly different than the expected number of minutes the crab remained buried in that zone (Kruskal–Wallis, $p = 0.05$) (Figure 4.7). There was no significant difference in the total time buried or the difference in the observed and expected number of minutes crabs were buried in the moderate or high EMF zones (Kruskal–Wallis, $p > 0.12$); (Figure 4.7). For the high EMF zone, the observed number of minutes was not significantly different from the expected number of minutes remaining buried because of the high variability (Kruskal–Wallis, $p = 0.12$) (Figure 4.7).

Table 4.1. Number of Observations of Crab Behavior and EMF Zone Location Based on 15-min Intervals for 72 hr

| Treatment | Behavior | EMF Zone | | | Total |
		Low	Moderate	High	
Control (5 crabs)	Buried	459	609	44	1112
	Active or resting	234	78	19	331
	Total	**693**	**687**	**63**	**1443**
EMF exposed (5 crabs)	Buried	141	653	118	912
	Active or resting	394	102	33	529
	Total	**535**	**755**	**151**	**1441**
Total Observations		**1228**	**1442**	**214**	**2884**

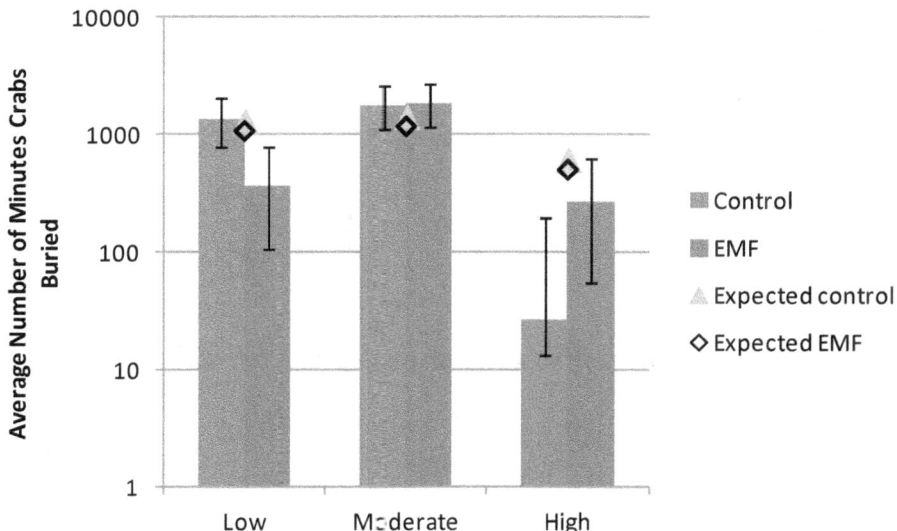

Figure 4.7. Average Number of Minutes Crabs Were Buried in Sediment in the Control and EMF-Exposed Tanks (±95% confidence interval) (*n* = 5 per tank). The expected number of minutes based on the proportional area of each zone for the control and EMF-exposed tanks is also shown.

In addition to the total time buried, we examined behavioral responses as measured by the number of times specific behaviors changed between buried, resting, and active (e.g., standing, walking, climbing). The number of times crabs changed behavior during the 3-day experiment was greater in the EMF-exposed tank compared to the control tank, but was not statistically significant (Kruskal–Wallis, p = 0.076). When the experiment was partitioned into 24-hr periods and the periods evaluated separately, both Day 1 and Day 2 had significantly more activity changes occurring in the EMF-exposed tank (Kruskal–Wallis, p < 0.05) compared to the control tank (Figure 4.8). By Day 3, the number of behavioral changes was not significantly different between the control tank and the EMF-exposed tank (Kruskal–Wallis, p = 0.35), although the number of change in activity by the EMF-exposed crabs was still greater. The power analysis estimated a sample size of 3 crabs would be needed to be able to detect a difference of 10 activities per day at 80 % power. Thus the statistical power for these tests was adequate (sample size used was 5).

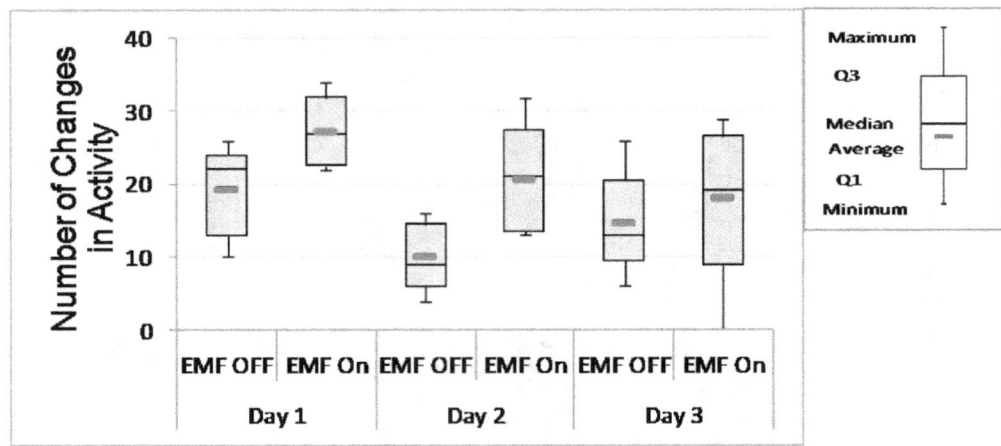

Figure 4.8. Number of Changes Between Behavioral Responses (buried, resting, active) for the Control (EMF off) and Treatment (EMF on) Tanks. Responses were evaluated on a 24-hr basis for the 3-day experiment.

Although the differences in the mean activity changes between control and EMF-exposed crabs became less significant by the third day of experimentation, the variability in crab behavior increased significantly during the 3 days in the EMF-exposed tank but not in the control tank (Figure 4.9) (regression, $p = 0.04$ and $p = 0.22$, respectively). The slopes associated with the percentage coefficient of variation of the number of changes in behavior were significantly different between the exposure treatments (regression, $p = 0.05$).

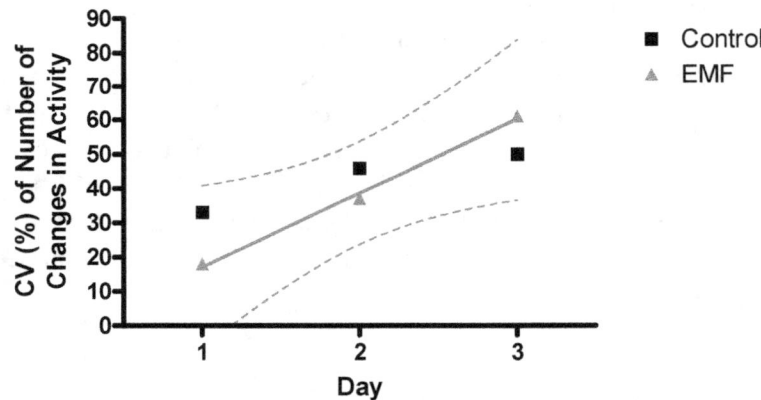

Figure 4.9. Percentage Coefficient of Variation (CV %) in Number of Activity Changes Through Time on a Daily Basis

4.5   Summary of FY 2011 Invertebrate Experiments

During FY 2011, EMF experiments focused on Dungeness crab as an important and representative bottom-dwelling decapod crustacean that could be exposed to MHK devices, particularly transmission cables. The results of these experiments are summarized in Table 4.2.

Table 4.2. Summary of EMF Experiments with Crustaceans During FY 2011

Experiment	Species Tested	Testing Endpoint	Result
EMF detection	Dungeness crab (Metacarcinus magister)	Antennular flicking response	No statistically significant detection of EMF observed (3 mT DC)
Food detection during EMF exposure	Dungeness crab (Metacarcinus magister)	Antennular flicking response	Ability to detect food after 20 hr of 3-mT DC EMF similar. Slight decrease in EMF-exposed crab compared to control, not statistically significant
		Feeding behaviors	Preliminary analysis suggests similarity between control and EMF-exposed crab
EMF avoidance/attraction	Dungeness crab (Metacarcinus magister)	Location observed active and resting	No significant difference between control and EMF-exposed (1 mT DC)
		Time buried in sand	Controls > EMF-exposed (1 mT DC) for first 48 hr
		Number of activity changes through time	EMF-exposed > control crabs for first 48 hr
		Variability in number of activity changes	EMF-exposed crabs activity variability increased through time

Initial tests measured the crabs' ability to sense EMF fields using the antennular flicking rate as a means of detection. Although the antennular flicking rate decreased slightly, it was not significantly different from the rate measured before EMF exposure. Likewise, the flicking rate response to a food odor decreased slightly after exposure to EMF; however, the difference was not statistically significant. Using the combined standard deviations from all control flicking rate data, the power analysis estimated sample sizes of 11 and 8 would be needed to be able to detect a difference of 10 flicks/min at 80 % power for the acute EMF exposures (Phase 1) and the food detection exposures (Phase 2), respectively. Thus the power for these tests was adequate; our minimum sample replication size was 23. The initial avoidance/attraction experiment shows some evidence of subtle changes in behavior (e.g., amount of time buried, number of changes and variability in activity through time). Additional replication is needed to further assess the behavioral responses.

4.6 FY 2012 Activities

Additional results from the preliminary avoidance/attraction will be analyzed at the beginning of FY 2012 to assess the influence of tidal stage, upstream and downstream positions in the tanks, and diel cycles on response activity. Crabs are known to respond to changes in chemical cues associated with tide changes (incoming vs. outgoing tides) and are generally more active at night. It is not known whether these responses and activities would be altered by EMF. For replication purposes, a second avoidance/attraction trial with the crab will be conducted during FY 2012. In addition, avoidance/attraction experiments with another crustacean, the American lobster, in FY 2012 will provide additional information on marine crustacean responses to upper-bounding EMF conditions. The experimental design will be based on results from the Dungeness crab exposures and prior knowledge of lobster habitat and behavior.

5.0 Discussion of Potential EMF Effects and FY 2012 Activities

A review of published studies that assessed the potential for adverse effects related to EMF exposure made it apparent that much of the available information was either not directly related to marine and estuarine settings or provided inconclusive or contradictory findings (Schultz et al. 2010). In some instances, experimental designs were not robust, and equipment limitations resulted in EMF exposures that were estimated or inferred. Because published EMF literature often contained uncertainties related to the actual EMF exposure or dose used during experiments, key investments were made at the beginning of this project to acquire a Helmholtz coil system that would produce a steady, uniform, and measurable EMF to support laboratory fish and invertebrate testing. As described in Section 2, this system enabled the project team to work with uniform magnetic fields ranging from 0.1 to 3 mT, and allowed a range of exploratory experiments to be conducted. These experiments included exposures occurring at the higher end of what might occur in a realistic field setting but that were found in some of the published literature, thereby providing an upper bounding-limit estimate of responses.

To better understand the potential effects of MHK in marine, estuarine, and freshwater environments, the project team chose test species that were considered 1) reasonable surrogates for threatened and endangered species, or those with ecological, commercial or recreational importance; 2) likely to encounter MHK devices or power cables during part or all of their life cycle; and 3) an integral component of a complex food web present in coastal environments. This approach enabled us to select reasonable environmental surrogates and develop tests that reflected likely exposure regimes. As described in Sections 3 and 4, selected fish and invertebrate species meeting these criteria were chosen for environmental effects testing during FY 2010–FY 2011.

Based on the available literature, acute effects including death from EMF exposure were not expected to occur. Therefore, testing focused on sublethal endpoints:

- organism growth and development (e.g., egg development, larval-to-juvenile metamorphosis, and parr-to-smolt transformation)

- physiological changes (e.g., stress hormones)

- behavioral responses (e.g., detection of EMF, interference with prey detection, avoidance or attraction to EMF).

For developmental and physiological tests, species were acquired from aquaculture or related facilities where organism age, condition, and previous exposure were known in order to reduce potential confounding test factors. For behavioral testing of crustaceans, experimental organisms acquired from the field shortly before testing were selected as most representative of a potential native population's behavioral response to an EMF exposure. These combined endpoints provide a broad picture of potential EMF effects from ocean energy devices that could affect important aquatic species. They also provide a body of knowledge that can be used to inform regulatory and stakeholder concerns regarding MHK pilot- or full-scale deployment projects.

EMF experiments with fish included species common to marine, estuarine, and freshwater environments. Juvenile salmonids were tested using a behavioral endpoint to determine if EMF exposure would decrease their ability to successfully evade predators, under the scenario that juvenile fish inhabiting nearshore locations could encounter MHK transmission cables. Tests were patterned after work by NOAA fisheries and others (Stone et al. 1994; Brown and Smith 1997; Scholz et al. 2000; Tierney et al. 2006) that assessed the effect of trace metals in stormwater on the predator response ability. Although the salmonid alarm response endpoint was inconclusive, concurrent exposure marker experiments showed no evidence of stress as measured by levels of cortisol in juvenile salmon. Decreases in melatonin levels, involved in smoltification of salmonids (Gern et al. 1984), were observed, however were not statistically significant.

Developmental experiments using rainbow trout addressed the potential exposure of fertilized eggs to transmission cables in riverine settings. There was no apparent affect on fertilization success rate. Although not statistically significant, exposure of fertilized trout eggs to EMF for extended periods appeared to delay the rate of egg development. Rainbow trout are also being used as a test organism by researchers at Oak Ridge National Laboratory for EMF, assessing alternative exposure mechanisms and end points.

Halibut were chosen as model surrogate flatfish that could be exposed to EMF directly from MHK devices during their pelagic (open water) lifestage as well as exposed to transmission cables after metamorphosis and settlement on the bottom. Flatfish metamorphosis is a complex and important component of growth and survival that has been well established for many years (Gisbert et al. 2002; Saele et al. 2003). As an example, one of the stages of halibut development involves transitioning between larval forms with eyes on both sides of the body to juvenile forms with eyes on one side of the body (Saele et al. 2003). It was therefore possible to adapt the well-understood life history staging protocols to assess EMF exposure. Experiments with Atlantic halibut suggested that a high EMF exposure may have reduced both growth and development in early life stages, although neither was statistically different from the controls. Experiments with California halibut showed no change in growth or development.

Dungeness crabs were chosen as a representative bottom-dwelling crustacean, inhabiting a wide-ranging coastline from the Gulf of Alaska to California. This commercially and recreationally important specie forages on bivalves, crustaceans and fish in estuarine, nearshore and offshore coastal waters, and may encounter EMF transmission cables. Initial tests were designed to assess whether crab could detect EMF fields by measuring a sensory receptor response, the antennular flicking rate before and during an acute EMF exposure. Similar to tests discussed above, these experiments were based on a previous body of work and protocols that examined antennular flicking rate in Dungeness crab as a quantitative measure of chemosensory acuity in the water column for food extracts (Pearson et al. 1979), petroleum hydrocarbons (Pearson et al. 1980, 1981) and salinity (Sugarman et al. 1983). The antennules are involved primarily in recognition of chemical signatures in the water column. However, other stimuli such as vibration and sound are known to elicit a flicking response. During EMF exposure, antennular flicking rate decreased slightly but was not significantly different from rates measured before EMF exposure. Likewise, the flicking rate response to a food odor decreased slightly after exposure to EMF, but was not statistically significant. Initial avoidance/attraction experiments have shown some evidence of subtle changes in behavior (e.g., amount of time buried, number of changes and variability in activity through time). However, these results are preliminary, and replication of the experiments and further analysis of the data are warranted to understand their meaning.

Experiments with additional species of interest to regulatory agencies and stakeholder groups (e.g., American lobster, elasmobranch species) will be conducted in FY 2012 to augment existing results and extend the body of scientific evidence regarding potential responses and effects of EMF exposure on aquatic organisms.

6.0 References

Bjornsson BT, SO Stefansson, and SD McCormick. 2011. Environmental endocrinology of salmon smoltification. *General and Comparative Endocrinology* 170(2):290–298.

Brown GE and RJF Smith. 1997. Conspecific skin extracts elicit antipredator responses in juvenile rainbow trout (*Oncorhynchus mykiss*). *Canadian Journal of Zoology* 75(11):1916–1922.

Brown KH, IR Schultz, and JJ Nagler. 2007. Reduced embryonic survival in rainbow trout resulting from paternal exposure to the environmental estrogen 17 alpha-ethynylestradiol during late sexual maturation. *Reproduction* 134(5):659–666.

Cada GF, MS Bevelheimer, KP Reimer, and JW Turner. 2011. *Effects on Freshwater Organisms of Magnetic Fields Associated with Hydrokinetic Turbines*. ORNL/TM-2011/244, Oak Ridge National Laboratory, Oak Ridge, Tennessee.

Chapman PF, M Crane, J Wiles, F Noppert, and E McIndoe. 1996. Improving the quality of statistics in regulatory ecotoxicity tests. *Ecotoxicology* 5:169–186.

CMACS. 2003. *A Baseline Assessment of Electromagnetic Fields Generated by Offshore Windfarm Cables*. COWRIE Report EMF – 01-2002 66, prepared for Collaborative Offshore Wind Research into the Environment Ltd. (COWRIE) by the Centre for Marine and Coastal Studies, University of Liverpool, United Kingdom.

Cochran WG and GM Cox. 1957. *Experimental Design*. John Wiley & Sons, Inc., New York.

Devaux A, F Luc, G Christian, and S Bony. 2011. Reproduction impairment following paternal genotoxin exposure in brown trout (*Salmo trutta*) and Arctic charr (*Salvelinus alpinus*). *Aquatic Toxicology* 101(2):405–411.

Gern W, WW Dickhoff, and LC Folmar. 1984. Increases in plasma melatonin titers accompanying seawater adaptation of coho salmon (*Oncorhynchus-kisutch*). *General and Comparative Endocrinology* 55(3):458–462.

Gill AB, Y Huang, I Gloyne-Phillips, J Metcalfe, V Quayle, J Spencer, and V Wearmouth. 2009. *COWRIE 2.0 Electromagnetic Fields (EMF) Phase 2: EMF-sensitive fish response to EM emissions from sub-sea electricity cables of the type used by the offshore renewable energy industry*. COWRIE-EMF-1-106, Collaborative Offshore Wind Research into the Environment Ltd., United Kingdom.

Gisbert E, G Merino, JB Muguet, D Bush, RH Piedrahita, and DE Conklin. 2002. Morphological development and allometric growth patterns in hatchery-reared California halibut larvae. *Journal of Fish Biology* 61:1217–1229.

Hellinger J and KP Hoffmann. 2009. Magnetic field perception in the Rainbow Trout, *Oncorhynchus mykiss*. *Journal of Comparative Physiology A – Neuroethology, Sensory, Neural, and Behavioral Physiology* 195(9):873–879.

Juutilainen J. 2005. Developmental effects of electromagnetic fields. *Bioelectromagnetics* S107–S115.

Lerchl A, A Zachmann, MA Ali, and RJ Reiter. 1998. The effects of pulsing magnetic fields on pineal melatonin synthesis in a teleost fish (brook trout, *Salvelinus fontinalis*). *Neuroscience Letters* 256(3):171–173.

Pearson WH, PC Sugarman, and DL Woodruff. 1979. Thresholds for detection and feeding behavior in the dungeness crab, *Cancer magister* (Dana). *Journal of Experimental Marine Biology and Ecology* 39(1):65–78.

Pearson WH, DL Woodruff, PC Sugarman, and BL Olla. 1980. Detection of petroleum hydrocarbons by the Dungeness crab, *Cancer magister*. *Fishery Bulletin* 78(3):821–826.

Pearson WH, PC Sugarman, DL Woodruff, and BL Olla. 1981. Impairment of the chemosensory antennular flicking response in the Dungeness crab, *Cancer magister*, by petroleum hydrocarbons. *Fishery Bulletin* 79(4):641–647.

Reiter RJ. 1995. Reported biological consequences related to the suppression of melatonin by electric and magnetic field exposure. *Integrative Physiological and Behavioral Science* 30(4):314–330.

Sæle Ø, JS Solbakken, K Watanabe, K Hamre, D Power, and K Pittman. 2004. Staging of Atlantic halibut (*Hippoglossus hippoglossus* L.) from first feeding through metamorphosis, including cranial ossification independent of eye migration. *Aquaculture* 239(1–4):445–465.

Schultz IR, A Skillman, JM Nicolas, DG Cyr, and JJ Nagler. 2003. Short-term exposure to 17 alpha-ethynylestradiol decreases the fertility of sexually maturing male rainbow trout (*r*). *Environmental Toxicology and Chemistry* 22(6):1272–1280.

Schultz IR, KH Brown, and JJ Nagler. 2008. Effect of parental exposure to trenbolone and the brominated flame retardant BDE-47 on fertility in rainbow trout (*Oncorhynchus mykiss*). *Marine Environmental Research* 66(1):47–49.

Schultz IR, DL Woodruff, KE Marshall, WJ Pratt, and G Roesijadi. 2010. *Effects of Electromagnetic Fields on Fish and Invertebrates. Task 2.1.3: Effects on Aquatic Organisms – Fiscal Year 2010 Progress Report.* PNNL-19883, Pacific Northwest National Laboratory, Richland, Washington.

Scholz NL, NK Truelove, BL French, BA Berejikian, TP Quinn, E Casillas, and TK Collier. 2000. Diazinon disrupts antipredator and homing behaviors in Chinook salmon (*Oncorhynchus tshawytscha*). *Canadian Journal of Fisheries and Aquatic Sciences* 57(9):1911–1918.

Skauli KS, JB Reitan, and BT Walther. 2000. Hatching in zebrafish (*Danio rerio*) embryos exposed to a 50 Hz magnetic field. *Bioelectromagnetics* 21(5):407–410.

Stevens RG and S Davis. 1996. The melatonin hypothesis: Electric power and breast cancer. *Environmental Health Perspectives* 104:135–140.

Sugarman PC, WH Pearson, and DL Woodruff. 1983. Salinity detection and associated behavior in the Dungeness crab, *Cancer magister*. *Estuaries* 6(4):380–386.

Stone SL and CB Schreck. 1994. Behavioral responses of juvenile coho salmon (*Oncorhynchus kisutch*) to pulp mill effluents. *Bulletin of Environmental Contamination and Toxicology* 53(3):355–359.

Tierney KB, AL Taylor, PS Ross, and CJ Kennedy. 2006. The alarm reaction of coho salmon parr is impaired by the carbamate fungicide IPBC. *Aquatic Toxicology* 79(2):149–157.

Wiltschko W and R Wiltschko. 2005. Magnetic orientation and magnetoreception in birds and other animals. *Journal of Comparative Physiology A – Neuroethology, Sensory, Neural, and Behavioral Physiology* 191(8):675–693.

www.ingramcontent.com/pod-product-compliance
Lightning Source LLC
Chambersburg PA
CBHW081425280526
45788CB00009B/3225